"Roxanne, Don't Go Yet."

What should she do? It was wonderful to be held in his arms, and yet . . . something warned her that if he kissed her, it would be no ordinary kiss.

Todd stood in the April moonlight and waited, as though there were all the time in the world. He gazed into her eyes, holding back nothing of himself and letting her read in his face his pain, his anger, his disillusionment.

"You scare me," she whispered. "You expect too much."

He turned his head slightly and brushed his lips against hers. "I'll never take more than you want to give."

KATE MERIWETHER
lives in Texas and is the mother of three sons. The major interest in her life is "people and what makes them tick." In her writing she is more concerned with characterization than with anything else.

Dear Reader,

Silhouette Special Editions are an exciting new line of contemporary romances from Silhouette Books. Special Editions are written specifically for our readers who want a story with heightened romantic tension.

Special Editions have all the elements you've enjoyed in Silhouette Romances and *more*. These stories concentrate on romance in a longer, more realistic and sophisticated way, and they feature greater sensual detail.

I hope you enjoy this book and all the wonderful romances from Silhouette.

Karen Solem
Editor-in-Chief
Silhouette Books

KATE MERIWETHER
Strictly Business

Silhouette Special Edition

Published by Silhouette Books New York

America's Publisher of Contemporary Romance

Silhouette Books by Kate Meriwether

Sweet Adversity (SE #89)
The Courting Game (SE #144)
Strictly Business (SE #179)

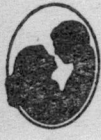
SILHOUETTE BOOKS, a Division of Simon & Schuster, Inc.
1230 Avenue of the Americas, New York, N.Y. 10020

Distributed by Pocket Books

ISBN: 0-671-53679-6

First Silhouette Books printing July, 1984

10 9 8 7 6 5 4 3 2 1

Map by Ray Lundgren

America's Publisher of Contemporary Romance

Printed in the U.S.A.

To Lisa

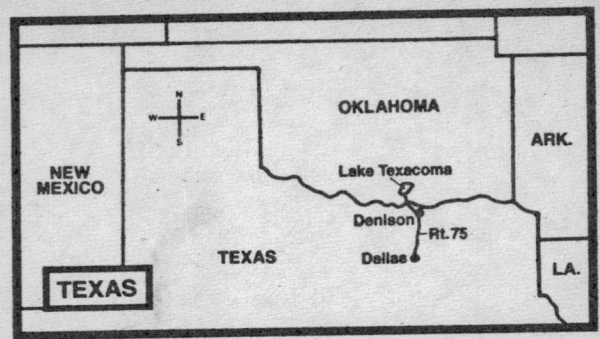

TEXAS

NEW MEXICO

OKLAHOMA

ARK.

Lake Texacoma

Denison

Rt. 75

TEXAS

Dallas

LA.

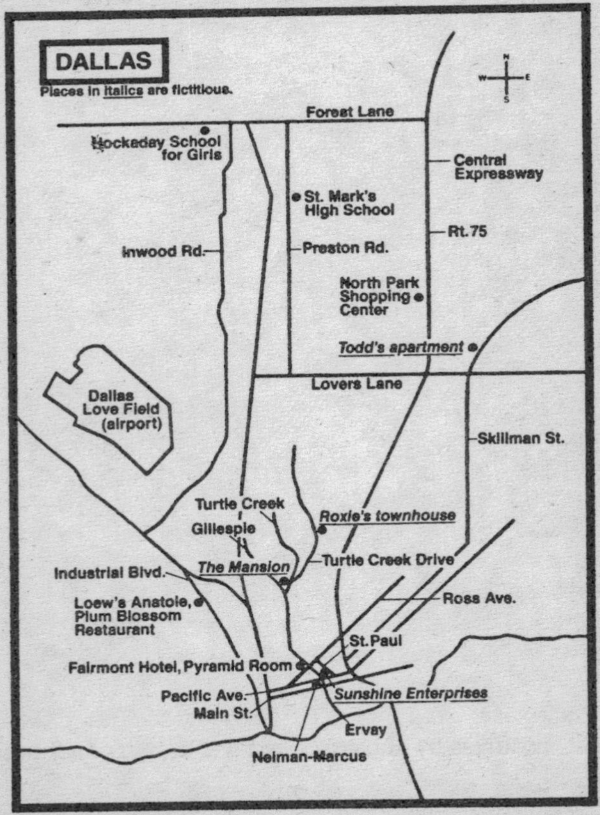

DALLAS

Places in *italics* are fictitious.

Forest Lane

Hockaday School for Girls

Central Expressway

St. Mark's High School

Rt. 75

Inwood Rd.

Preston Rd.

North Park Shopping Center

Todd's apartment

Lovers Lane

Dallas Love Field (airport)

Skillman St.

Turtle Creek

Roxie's townhouse

Gillespie

Turtle Creek Drive

Industrial Blvd.

The Mansion

Loew's Anatole, Plum Blossom Restaurant

Ross Ave.

St. Paul

Fairmont Hotel, Pyramid Room

Pacific Ave.

Sunshine Enterprises

Main St.

Ervay

Neiman-Marcus

Chapter One

The elevator whooshed to the twentieth floor of the new First City Center in downtown Dallas and deposited Roxanne Lyons in the spacious reception area of Sunshine Enterprises. As usual she was a little late getting back from lunch and a little breathless from the rush. Not that it mattered, though. She would probably still be working at 10:00 P.M. A confirmed workaholic, she thrived on long hours and hard work. Still, to keep up the pace she needed a break in the middle of the day. Sometimes she spent her lunch hour on a business deal, and that was exhilarating, too. Today, though, she had recharged her batteries by trying on dresses in the Designer Shop at Neiman-Marcus.

She was already wondering why she had bought another dress by Halston when she already had three hanging in her closet that hadn't been worn in months. But she didn't have one in that gorgeous shade of teal that did such wonders for her eyes. Surely she could find an occasion to wear it.

Roxanne breezed past the receptionist with a quick wave, calling over her shoulder, "Neiman's is going to deliver some packages later this afternoon. Just send them on back, will you?"

She hurried back to her private office with a quick greeting to Lorraine Thompson, the secretary she shared with her father, president of Sunshine Enterprises. "Let me grab a quick cup of coffee, Lorraine, and we'll get started on that Scottsdale proposal."

Lorraine muttered something about too much caffeine, which Roxie conveniently chose not to hear. Lorraine was a fantastic secretary and a kind, wonderful person. Roxie wished that she didn't have such an overdeveloped maternal instinct, but nobody was perfect. Every day Lorraine grumbled at Roxie about too much caffeine and not enough rest, and every day Roxie ignored her.

Roxanne poured a cup of scalding black coffee and went into her washroom to freshen up while the coffee cooled. Her thick, tawny hair needed a good brushing after the Texas wind had tossed it about, and she touched her long lashes with another dab of mascara. Otherwise her daisy-fresh good looks were intact, her skin glowing and her smile brilliant. She'd never been happier.

She went back into her office and sat down on one of the white chairs to catch her breath for a moment. She sipped her coffee and wished she'd taken time to eat something. "Lorraine," she called to her secretary in the outer office, "do you happen to have any crackers out there?"

"Of course," Lorraine answered, coming in at once with crackers, cheese spread and an apple. "Thank goodness you're going to eat something. I worry about the way you skip meals. Here," she said, spreading cheese on the crackers and handing Roxie a paper plate. "All the money in the world and you don't eat any better than a starving child in Calcutta!"

"Oh, Lorraine, you know the rich are supposed to be fashionably thin," Roxie said, smiling. She didn't lose much time devouring the cheese and crackers, however, to Lorraine's gratification.

"You get much thinner and you'll look like a scarecrow," Lorraine scolded. "Don't you know men prefer a woman with some meat on her bones?"

"Now, Lorraine," Roxie objected in amusement. "My weight is perfect for my height, and no man has complained about my looks since I was twelve years old."

"Well, I'm sure your dad thinks you're too skinny."

"Oh, pooh, if you and Dad had your way, I'd be a little butterball."

"I bet you don't weigh a hundred pounds."

"For heaven's sake, Lorraine, I'm only five foot three. And believe me, on my frame every *ounce* shows." Roxanne was elegantly slim and small boned, and thanks to an abundance of nervous energy, she had little trouble keeping trim. No need to take chances with fat, though, she thought, chomping on the apple, especially when her bone structure offered no place to hide it.

The intercom buzzed and Lorraine went back to her

desk to answer it, returning after a brief interval with a dismayed look on her face. "Your dad wants you to come into his office right away," she said. "And he sounds madder than a wet hen."

"What is it this time?"

"He didn't say."

"Hummm." Roxanne cast her eyes to the ceiling and continued to chomp on the apple. "Let me think . . . it's Friday, so there weren't any conferences this morning. Did he have an appointment at lunch?"

Lorraine was distressed that Roxie pondered the calendar rather than hurry to her father's office. Of course, Roxie hadn't heard him bellowing on the telephone, so maybe she didn't understand that it was urgent. "Roxie, he wants you right away," she pleaded.

"I'm going, I'm going." Roxie swallowed the last of her coffee. "You didn't answer me. Did he have an appointment at lunch?"

"No—no, he didn't. He left early and went over to the gym."

"I don't see what could have upset him at the gym. Are you sure he didn't say what's wrong?"

"All he said was for you to get over there right now before the whole place falls apart." Lorraine's distress was genuine. She was very fond of her employer and his daughter, and anything which upset them upset Lorraine, too.

"Oh, don't worry about it, Lorraine," Roxie said with a shrug. "You know how Dad exaggerates everything. Maybe he couldn't bench-press more than two hundred pounds today."

"Roxie, please, I know it's something terrible. I never heard him shout like that before. Please go see what's wrong before he works himself into a stroke."

Roxie set down her coffee cup with a clatter. Lorraine really should have been a nurse the way she worried over everyone's health. Still, she didn't get excited very often. Maybe there was something wrong. But what could it be, when everything had been going so well?

Roxanne knew the minute she stepped inside her father's sun-filled office that Lorraine was right. George Lyons was a man given to quick outbursts of temper, yet Roxie had never seen him in such high dudgeon. His thick white hair was in perfect contrast to the livid red of his complexion, and he was pacing the floor with a sheaf of papers clutched in his fist, muttering curses. Roxie spent one brief moment feeling sorry for the person who had riled her father and then went into the "daddy's girl" role that she had played all her life to placate his bad moods.

"Now, Dad," she said soothingly, "sit down and let me get you a cup of coffee."

"Coffee!" he shouted. "It's going to take a fifth of whiskey to calm me down this time."

Roxie quietly proceeded to pour a cup of steaming coffee. "Come sit down," she urged, lowering herself to the soft leather couch and patting the seat beside her.

George paced a few more steps, then flopped onto the couch and took a big swig of the coffee. Grabbing his throat and jumping to his feet, he yelled, "Damn it, Roxie. First you wreck my business, then you try to scald me. What have I ever done to make you hate me so much?" He rushed to the bar in the corner of his office and popped an ice cube into his mouth, then glowered at Roxie from across the room.

She had no idea what was wrong with him, but she knew her father well enough to know that she would soon find out. She leaned back against the leather and helped herself to a sip of coffee from his mug, ignoring his angry stare. Finally she smiled at him and patted the couch again.

"Come tell me about it," she said.

He knew the affection in her voice was genuine. He grumbled again, but the worst was over. He sat down beside her, and Roxanne leaned over and squeezed his hand.

"Is something wrong, Daddy?"

He uttered a bitter laugh. "Is something wrong? You bet there is." He pushed his big, gnarled fingers through his hair, so it stood in spikes.

"I just don't see how the whole world can come to an end that fast. Everything was fine this morning."

"No, it wasn't. You just didn't know any different."

"Daddy, I saw you right before lunch and you were fine."

"I didn't know any different then, either." His hand moved down to massage his chest.

"So whatever it is, it's happened since lunch?" Roxie was totally perplexed. "The sky fell in while I was shopping at Neiman's?"

"I hope you got something pretty, because it's probably the last time you'll have money." George sighed with self-pity.

This was serious. Never in Roxie's entire life had George acted like their money supply was anything but inexhaustible. The more Roxie spent, the more there was to spend. She suddenly wished that she had bought an Oscar de la Renta ballgown instead of an Ultrasuede shirtdress that she didn't even want—if it were really to be her final purchase. But it couldn't be *that* serious . . . could it?

"Dad, why don't you just tell me what's happened. I'm scaring myself to death trying to imagine."

"Do you know what day this is?" George gave her a hard look.

"Well, of course. It's Friday."

"No, no, no. The date."

Roxie's brow furrowed. "March 30th, I think."

"Wrong. It's the 31st."

Roxie shrugged. What was the significance of the date?

"March 31st, Roxie, don't you understand?" He wondered how she could be so dense. "March 31st. The last day of the quarter."

"The last—oh." The last day of the financial period. So there must be bad news about the company's profits. Puzzling . . . things had seemed to be booming. "Have you gotten the financial reports already? The quarter isn't over until midnight."

"I had Accounting work up some preliminary reports," George answered, poking the sheaf of papers at her. "We'll get the final figures next week."

"Does it look bad?"

"*Bad?* It's disastrous!"

Roxie twisted the emerald ring on her slender finger and peered into her father's troubled face. Their eyes met, but George couldn't bring himself to smile. He was too miserable.

"Now, Daddy," she murmured, patting his hand, "I know you'll figure out something. It's not the end of the world."

"Oh, yes, it is," he protested. "The end of my world, anyway, with my baby girl working alongside me." He'd been so glad to have her come home to join his business, and she'd been such a help. He never dreamed that she'd threaten the corporate empire he'd spent his life's blood building.

Roxie jumped to her feet. "Daddy!" she cried. "Don't talk that way. Tell me what's wrong!"

"If you'll look at these financial statements, you can see for yourself," he answered, handing her the computer printouts. "Look at the bottom line for each division of the company."

Roxie's eye quickly scanned the columns of figures for the four divisions of Sunshine Enterprises. Her own Finance Division was solidly in the black, but the Development Division was off 25 percent from the previous quarter, and both Acquisitions and Marketing were off a full 50 percent. "Why, Dad, this is awful," she cried. "Losses for this period are nearly a quarter of a million dollars."

George slumped in the corner of the couch, his head in his hands.

"I don't understand," she said, pacing the floor exactly as her father had done previously. "All the weekly reports have sounded pretty good." She tossed the printouts on her father's desk as though she could toss away the financial disaster they contained. "There's been nothing to warn us this was happening."

George shook his head. "Yes, there was, Roxie, but I ignored it."

She dropped to her knees beside him. "What was it?" she asked.

"It started when you moved back from Chicago," he said mournfully. "Everything was fine until last quarter. But you joined the company in January and took over the Finance Division, and everything just went to pot after that."

"Dad, that's not fair," she protested. "My division made a healthy profit, 10 percent more than last quarter."

"Sure, *your* division did OK. But look what happened to Acquisitions and Marketing."

"Dad, *I* don't run those divisions." She knew her father was a flinty businessman whose judgments could be severe, and she didn't intend to be blamed for something that wasn't her fault.

"No, of course not. But ever since you came, *nobody* has run those divisions—because those jackasses in charge of them have been too busy going ga-ga over you."

"What?"

"You heard me. Julian and Rusty haven't been able to keep their minds on business because they've been following you around like lost puppy dogs."

"Well, they've been underfoot a lot, but I've gotten *my* work done. I supposed they had, too."

"I watched them making fools of themselves, but I didn't realize it had gotten so far out of hand. You remember when you went to Phoenix and Rusty went with you? He lost out on a good deal in Cozumel that cost us lots of money. And then Julian went to Lake Tahoe with you and lost out on a big development here in Dallas. That cost us another fortune."

"Dad, I went to Phoenix and Lake Tahoe on business, to work out the financing on resort developments that earned us a big profit."

"Sure, you went on business, but those guys went because they were infatuated with you."

"That's not my fault."

"Yes, it is. You flirt with them."

"Daddy, I'd flirt with a chair if it was the only thing in the room to flirt with. It doesn't mean a thing."

"Not to you, maybe. But it messed up their judgment."

Roxie had no patience with incompetence. To her the solution was very simple. "Well, you'll just have to fire them, then."

"What!" George exclaimed. "Fire two VP's who have been with me since they were college boys, over ten years? They know this company inside out. Why, I hate to admit it, but I'm totally dependent on them. I *can't* fire them."

"You'll have to, if they don't have any better judgment than that."

"Roxie, how can you be so cold-blooded?" George cried indignantly.

"I guess I learned it from you," she responded, bristling. "How many times have you sat at the dinner table and talked about firing some employee because he was incompetent?"

"That was a long time ago," he answered, waving aside her comment. "I'm not that hotheaded any more. I found out the hard way that you can't afford

to fire a valuable executive because of one mistake."
George took Roxie's face in his gnarled fingers and
sighed. "Roxie, if I lose them, I'll have to shut down
the company. I'm too old to start training somebody
else."

"Then what do you propose to do?"

"Send you back to the bank in Chicago and go back
to taking care of the financial matters myself. I can
take care of most of it. I did it before you came home
and I can do it again. But I just can't do the
Acquisitions and Marketing myself. I'm too old.
Takes a young person with lots of energy to do that."

Roxie stood up, her jaw sagging in disbelief.
"You'd send *me,* your own *daughter,* back to Chicago
in order to keep those two lunkheads?" Her temper
burst loose. She stormed around the office, knocking
things out of the way and shouting angry accusations
that made George wince.

When she finally wore herself out, George lum-
bered to his feet and put his arms around her. "There,
there, baby girl," he crooned. "Everything is going to
be just fine."

Roxie cast a murderous glance at him, but she was
too drained to work herself into another temper fit.

"Daddy, I had a perfectly good job in Chicago. I
got my MBA, I went through the bank's executive
training program and then I headed up my own
division in corporate finance. I had lots of friends and
a beautiful apartment. But then Mama died and you
were all alone, so I came back to Dallas to be with
you. It was time for me to start learning about the
company so I can take it over when you retire. And I
can honestly say the last three months have been the

happiest time of my life. I love working for your company, helping to build something that's going to be mine someday. There wasn't that kind of opportunity at the bank. I'm *not* leaving Dallas. I'm your daughter and you can't get rid of me!"

"I don't want to get rid of you, Roxie—but I don't want to watch Sunshine Enterprises go down the tubes, either."

"All you have to do is fire two VP's and the company will be right back in the black."

George stretched out his arms in appeal. "Roxie, I can't fire them, don't you understand? They're good officers, both of them. I can't blame them for running after you. I would have done the same thing myself at their age. You're the kind of woman who would turn any man's head."

Roxie dropped onto the sofa with a doleful grin. "I don't know if that's a compliment or an insult."

"All you have to do is look in the mirror." George was quite proud of his daughter's beauty, but he'd never expected it to backfire like this.

Roxie smiled. The storm was over, and it looked as if she had won. Her father didn't know it yet, but he wouldn't send her back to Chicago. "Put on your thinking cap, Daddy, because you've got to find a way to get Julian and Rusty to act like VP's again."

George groaned. "There's no way, not as long as you're here and single and flirting with them every day."

"I'll stop flirting."

They looked at each other and burst out laughing. "Well, I'll *try* to stop flirting," she amended.

"Won't do any good," George argued. "As long as

you're single and available, they're going to try to win your hand."

Roxie crossed one elegant leg over the other. "I suppose I could get married. That would put an end to it."

"What kind of solution is that? You've never settled down to one man in your life."

"No, but I'm twenty-seven years old. It's time I did. I'm sure I can find an ambitious man who'd like to help me run this company someday."

"Roxie, don't be crazy. Someday you'll find some nice young man and fall in love—just like your mother and I did—and *then* you can get married. Not until." His look was stern.

Roxie rested her head against the back of the couch and ignored her father's admonition. Silly, absent-minded Daddy, she thought, he's getting sentimental in his old age. He's forgotten that he and Mama married to consolidate their real estate holdings and fell in love afterward. Roxie's mind focused on the problem at hand and raced to find a way out of the dilemma. "Wait, Daddy, what did you say a few minutes ago? That as long as I'm single, they're going to try to win my hand?"

George nodded.

"Well, don't you see? That's our answer. We'll have a contest, and I'll marry the one who can earn the highest profits in a six-month period."

"Roxie, have you lost your ever-loving mind? You can't just marry yourself off to . . . to the . . . highest bidder."

"What difference does it make? I have to marry *somebody,* and it would be better to marry someone who can help me run the company when you're gone."

"Roxie! You're putting the cart before the horse. *First* comes love, *then* comes marriage."

"Love, pooh! I've never been in love in my life."

"That's only because you haven't been lucky enough to meet the right man. Give yourself time. It'll happen sooner or later."

"When I'm forty and the company has crumbled into ashes? No, thanks, Daddy. I'm going to get married in six months, to whichever one of these guys can make us the most money."

"Roxie, stop talking like this! I forbid it!"

She rose and walked behind the couch, leaning over to drop a kiss onto his white hair. "Daddy, did I ever tell you about the psychological test they gave me at the bank? I scored in the ninety-fifth percentile on ambition and aggressiveness—and *zero* on personal relations."

George looked up at her in disbelief. What on earth had happened to his sweet baby girl while she was in Chicago?

"It's true," she continued. "I like to flirt, but I'm really not interested in a serious relationship with a man. I'm too wrapped up in business, with making lots of money and getting to the top. So you see," she added, gently massaging the tension from his neck, "I'll never get married unless it's for the sake of the company, because that's all I really care about. It doesn't matter to me who it is. Rusty and Julian are both nice guys. Either one of them would be a good son-in-law to you. So it's settled."

George thought that the twentieth floor of the First

City Center must have tilted, the way his head was spinning. Roxie seemed like a stranger, not the same daughter who had charmed and teased and humored him all her life.

Roxie watched him stare into his coffee cup and felt confused. Ever since she was a child, she had used George for her example, doing her best to become just like him. Yet now he seemed dismayed to find the very traits in her which he'd prided in himself. Why didn't he welcome her eager effort to help him save the company?

George knew for sure that he didn't want to lose his daughter—but he didn't want to lose his company, either. He would never allow anything, not even Roxie, to wreck the company that was more dear to him than his own life. What to do, what to do? He walked to the window and looked down at the bustling traffic below moving in orderly fashion to the traffic signals. Should he try Roxie's plan? Was it possible to use her scheme to rescue his company and keep his daughter as well? He pressed his forehead against the cold window glass and tried to think.

Roxie came to stand beside him and leaned her tiny frame against his in a gentle hug. "I love this company as much as you do, Daddy. I want to help save it."

He turned with a sigh. "I don't think it will work, Roxie. In a two-man race, the loser will take defeat as something personal. I'm afraid he'd lose too much face and pull out of the company."

"Well, at least you'd keep one of the VP's. That's better than losing both of them."

George shook his head. "As a team, they're unbeatable. But they don't have the same strengths and weaknesses, so it takes both of them. I can't afford to lose either one."

Roxie wandered back to the counter and poured another cup of coffee. It looked as if the problem were unsolvable.

At that moment George brightened. "Of course, it might work if we broadened the contest. We could let all the VP's compete, not just Julian and Rusty. Then there would be several losers and nobody would take it personally."

Roxie considered. There were seven VP's, including herself. One snag, though . . . "Dad, how many of them are already married?"

George went down the list. "Bill Garner is married, and Wes Norton. That leaves Rusty, Julian, Hamlin Ayres, and Todd Kendrick. Well, four VP's will be enough for the contest."

"Todd Kendrick! Daddy, he's the biggest sourpuss in the world. I haven't seen him smile once in the three months I've been in Dallas."

"Oh, Todd's all right. Got divorced about six months ago and took it pretty hard. He won't win, anyway. Doesn't have his heart in his work right now."

"Why haven't you fired him, then?"

"Because he's one of the best people I've got. Just having a rough time, that's all. He'll get over it. And he's made me enough money in the past twelve years that I can afford to indulge him for a few months."

"Oh, Daddy," Roxie sputtered in exasperation. "Here you are with three VP's that ought to be fired, and you won't do it. Yet you'd package me up and ship me back to Chicago without a moment's hesitation. You men sure stick together!" She stood up and smoothed the wrinkles from the front of her plum-and-pewter plaid skirt.

George knew that it was time to change the subject. He had confidence in his business decisions, but somehow he didn't think Roxie would see them the same way. No need to get another battle raging when they had worked out a solution. Come to think of it, it was a perfect solution. It would get the VP's back to work, piling up profits to win Roxie's hand. Besides, all his top employees were super guys, and any one of them would make Roxie a wonderful husband. If she wasn't interested in picking out a husband for herself, she couldn't do better than one of the men he'd handpicked for his company. They were all winners, and she could easily fall in love with any one of them.

He smiled up at his lovely daughter. "I'll buy you a beach house in the Caribbean for your wedding present."

The air was charged with tension on the following Wednesday when the officers of Sunshine Enterprises met in the conference room for their regular monthly executive session. The financial report for the quarter had already been distributed, and everybody was uneasy. George Lyons was well-known for his hot temper, and all his VP's had experienced his wrath at one time or another. Today would probably be a real humdinger. George could get mad enough when the profit margin was only 5 percent. None of them could recall a time when there had been an actual *loss*.

They stood in small groups, talking quietly and waiting for their president. Rusty Wales and Julian

Mackley, the two VP's with disastrous losses in their divisions, stood alone, pariahs outcast by the group for fear they would bring bad luck to the others.

Julian had already checked the total in his profit-sharing account to see whether it was enough to support him until he could find another job. Not that he relished the thought of hunting for a job when he had a $100,000 quarterly loss on his record. With business generally in a slump, what other company would want him? If only he'd kept his mind on business, instead of tagging along behind Roxie Lyons. But she was such a gorgeous female, and he absolutely adored her.

Rusty Wales gnawed at his fingernail, a childhood habit that reappeared when he was under intolerable stress. This job had been his whole life, his family in a way, since George Lyons had more or less adopted him during his college days. Rusty's parents had died long ago, and George was like a father to him. Why, part of the reason for chasing after Roxie was in hopes of making George his real father. That was only part of the reason, though. The biggest part of it was her looks, her vivacity, her energy. Oh, how he wanted her! And now his profits were such a shambles that he'd never get her. He'd be lucky if she ever spoke to him again.

Todd Kendrick entered the room well after everyone else, the top button of his shirt unbuttoned and his tie askew. He was in no mood for small talk and tried to time his entrance to arrive just minutes before the president. He didn't even look up when someone spoke to him, and headed straight for the bar to mix himself a strong bourbon and water. He noticed that everyone else was drinking coffee. Cowards! They must be expecting George to be in a bad mood. So what if he was? Life couldn't possibly be any worse. It would be a relief to get fired, so Todd wouldn't have to drag himself down here every day to go through the motions. He groaned, running his fingers across his chin and trying to remember whether he had shaved this morning. Probably not, but it just didn't seem to matter. Nothing mattered these days. He pushed one hand through his thick golden-brown hair and realized that he probably needed a haircut, too. He took a chair at the conference table, the first officer to do so, and lowered his head and glared, the usual gold flecks now dead embers in his brown eyes. Come on, come on, he thought. Let's get this over with.

All conversation stopped when George Lyons entered the room, Roxie by his side. George went straight to the head of the table, nodding to the others to assume their places. He wasn't all smiles, but on the other hand, he didn't come in bellowing like a mad bull the way they had expected. Roxie made the rounds, greeting everyone with a smile, fluttering the hearts of even the married men. She could absolutely charm the paper off the wall when she took the notion.

Today she wore the teal-blue shirtwaist dress belted with a bright silk scarf. Her tawny shoulder-length hair hung in deep waves, curled on the ends. Her fingernails gleamed with coral nail polish that picked up the colors in her silk scarf, and the fragrance of lilies of the valley floated in the air around her. She was totally feminine—and totally business. As soon as her father pounded the table with his gavel, she was in her place, the financial reports in her hand.

George went over the routine business matters first, knowing that tension was building the longer he delayed discussion of the financial reports. In a fit of pure orneriness, George called on Rusty to make projections on marketing a condominium in Vail, Colorado, that had not yet been approved. And he made Julian squirm by inquiring about a land purchase in Acapulco that was still nothing more than a concept. When he had stretched everybody's nerves as far as he could, George broke the news about the contest.

Always a showman, he did it with a dramatic flair that had all of them on the edge of their seats. For a moment he thought that Bill Garner and Wes Norton might offer to divorce their wives in order to be eligible for the contest, but George quickly squelched that remote possibility by telling them that they were disqualified. George was beaming with happiness in the knowledge that his beloved daughter would be marrying one of these first-rate men, and when they got over their surprise, the men were all beaming, too. All except Todd Kendrick, but unfortunately nothing could make him smile these days. Todd leaned forward, clicking his pen impatiently and thinking what a harebrained scheme George had come up with this time. Why would any man in his right mind want to get tangled up with a spoiled little flirt like Roxie Lyons?

Hamlin Ayres tentatively raised his hand. "Gee, Mr. Lyons, I wouldn't want you to take it amiss, because I'm very fond of Roxie. You know that. But I just got engaged to Sybil Forrester, and—well, I just couldn't let her down." Before George could respond, Hamlin quickly added, "Of course, I want the best for the company, and I'll work just as hard as if I *were* in the contest."

George's eyes swept the conference table. Bill and Wes were frowning with disappointment to be left out of what looked like a great adventure. Hamlin was agitated, thinking that the boss might misunderstand and that his future with the company might be ruined. Todd was staring at the ceiling in total disinterest. Rusty and Julian were grinning from ear to ear, sizing up each other out of the corners of their eyes. This wasn't going the way George had planned. It had plainly become a two-man race, the very thing he wanted to avoid. Not much he could do about Hamlin at this point, since the guy had gone and gotten himself engaged. But maybe he could get Todd to show a little fight, enough to seem to be in the race—even though he was doomed to be a poor third. Now, what would it take to prick up his ears? George tried to remember what he had heard about Todd's divorce. Why was it his wife had left him? Oh, yes—she found a man with more money. Hummmm. George would sweeten the pot and see what happened.

"Well, fellows, this wraps up the meeting," he said. "We'll pursue negotiations on the Vail project and the Acapulco project. And in six months, when the second set of quarterly reports is in, the VP who shows the greatest profits for that period will receive the hand of my daughter in marriage." He paused for dramatic effect, then continued. "I think I forgot to mention that the winner will also receive 5 percent of the stock in Sunshine Enterprises in his own name. Stock is selling right now at $36 a share, and we have something like 750,000 shares outstanding, so that's a little wedding present worth about—figure that out for me, will you, Julian?"

They waited while Julian punched the figures into his calculator. He looked up with a surprised grin on his face. "That's over a million dollars, George— $1,350,000 to be exact."

George was happy. He had a deep affection for all these men, and it would be only proper for his daughter to marry a millionaire. "Of course, Roxie will also get 5 percent of the shares in her own name. And I told her I'd buy her a beach house in the Caribbean for a wedding present." He aimed a watchful glance in Todd's direction. Todd was still staring at the ceiling, his jaws clenched. He seemed to be in an agony of indecision now that so much money was at stake in the contest. In the hubbub of excitement, nobody else noticed him except George, who watched with satisfaction as Todd slowly lowered his chair to the floor and cast a skeptical look at Roxie. George had known Todd very well, for a very long time, and he knew how Todd's mind worked. George could read on Todd's face his decision to enter the race before it was ever voiced aloud.

Todd cleared his throat and spoke for the first time in the entire meeting. "When does the contest start, George?"

"Tomorrow morning," George answered with a kindly smile. It had worked. It would cost him a million dollars, but his scheme had worked. There were now three men in the race for his daughter's hand, and he would not only be able to keep his daughter, but all his valuable employees as well.

George turned to Roxie and lifted his coffee mug in a toast. "And may the best man win."

Chapter Two

Rusty pulled his sports car to the entry of Loew's Anatole, then opened the door for Roxie and handed the keys to the parking valet. He was proud to go inside the spectacular hotel complex with a good-looking woman like Roxie beside him. He liked it when heads turned to look at them.

He had never worked harder than he had during the past three days, trying to get ahead in the competition. But now it was the weekend and time to kick up his heels a little.

Roxie couldn't help feeling a little amused by Rusty's choice of restaurants. When he asked her to go out, she had suggested Chinese food, and Rusty had decided to impress her by choosing the Plum Blossom, one of several elegant—and expensive—restaurants in the hotel complex.

She was dressed in sleek black slacks topped by a silk tunic of narrow, brightly colored stripes that emphasized her vibrant skin coloring. A wide gold belt with an unusual butterfly clasp accented the curve of her tiny waist. Her tawny shoulder-length hair gleamed in the soft, incandescent lights, and her bubbling laughter and animated conversation drew all eyes in their direction as the waiter led them to their reserved table near the huge bronze statue of Buddha that dominated the room. The Chinese waiter brought goblets of ice water and left menus for their study.

"You look gorgeous tonight," Rusty said, beaming at her.

"Why, thank you, Rusty," she answered. She didn't do it on purpose, but her eyelashes fluttered just a little. Flirtation was as natural as breathing to Roxie, and as automatic.

Rusty sighed with bliss. He had to win this contest. It would be heaven to have Roxie beside him for the rest of his life, her glamour the proof of his masculinity. Only a real man could win a woman like Roxie, and Rusty would bask in the glow of other men's jealousy. On Monday he would redouble his efforts. He would work eighteen hours a day if necessary. But he must win.

There was only one small fly in the ointment: *Julian.* Rusty had a healthy respect for Julian. They had worked together as an unbeatable team for ten years. For every weakness Rusty had, Julian had a corresponding strength. And Julian knew Rusty's every vulnerability. Julian would be tough to beat. The thought roused a sense of competition that spurted adrenaline into Rusty's bloodstream. Yes, Julian would be tough to beat—but oh, how sweet would be the victory over a worthy opponent. The scent of battle stirred Rusty as it had the warriors of old. To defeat Julian would be just as exciting as to win Roxie—more so. His male sense of priorities prized the victory more than the reward. He covered Roxie's hand with his own and smiled into her eyes.

"I'm going to win this contest, Roxie. I just have to. I adore you."

"Well, of course you'll win, Rusty. You'll make so much money for the company that nobody will ever catch up with you." She gazed back at Rusty and thought of next month's profit and loss statements. She loved a financial statement with a bottom line in seven digits. If they concentrated all their energy, she and Rusty could make millions and millions of dollars. In fact, as young as they were, maybe billions. She turned her hand palm up in Rusty's and squeezed.

The waiter served crab claws with a hot soy sauce, then set up a firepot at their table and prepared soup by dropping such delicacies as quail eggs and slivers of fish and vegetables into a simmering chicken broth.

They sipped their steaming soup without talking, lost in their separate thoughts. Rusty daydreamed of himself as conquering warrior, Julian at his feet. Roxie contemplated a vault full of bundles and bundles of money. Their hands met and clung.

"Well, well, fancy meeting you here," said a familiar voice, breaking their reverie. They looked up to see Julian Mackley standing at their table, Lorraine Thompson at his side.

"What brings you to the Plum Blossom tonight?" Rusty asked irritably.

"Oh, I come here a lot. And Lorraine kindly agreed to accompany me tonight."

What was going on here? Lorraine was a very attractive woman, but she was at least twenty years older than Julian. This was obviously not an ordinary date. Roxie suspected that Julian and Lorraine were together because Lorraine was the person with access to Roxie's engagement calendar and knew where Roxie would be tonight. Could it be that Julian was spying on them? Roxie gave Julian a dazzling smile that pierced Rusty to the quick. But she couldn't help it. It was just too flattering to have two men fighting over her.

"You don't mind if we join you, do you?" asked Julian as he ushered Lorraine into a chair.

"We've already ordered," Rusty replied.

"We'll order the same thing you're getting. That'll make it easier on the waiter."

The waiter brought extra soup bowls and tried to be polite. Before he could serve the next course, the hearty voice of George Lyons made his presence known. He came down the aisle with Tammy Matthews, Rusty's secretary, in tow.

"What a big surprise," George boomed.

"Why, Dad, what brings you to the Plum Blossom?" Roxie asked, while the men jumped to their feet. "You don't even like Chinese food."

"Never too late to learn," he answered. "Tammy tells me this place comes highly recommended."

"I'll bet," Roxie muttered under her breath. This was too much. Tammy was at least thirty years younger than George, younger even than Roxie herself. Didn't Dad realize how ridiculous he looked? Roxie and Rusty exchanged perplexed glances.

"OK if we join you? Sit here, Tammy," George said, borrowing a chair from an adjoining table in his usual peremptory manner. He snapped his fingers at the waiter to bring another chair. "What's the matter with that waiter," he grumbled. "He looks like he just swallowed a persimmon."

"Maybe he thinks it would be easier to serve you if you had a separate table. We're half through our meal already." Roxie scooted her chair closer to Rusty's to make room for the newcomers.

"Nonsense," George objected. "We can skip the first course and have what you're having. That way we can all be together and catch up on the news. No secrets, now," he warned.

Tammy wilted under the look of betrayal Rusty shot her way. She had been his secretary ever since she got her associate's degree in secretarial science, and she had always been loyal to him. But what else could she do when the Big Boss ordered her to look at Rusty's calendar and see where he was taking Roxie tonight? Oh, my, she certainly hoped Rusty would forgive her. But she had no choice except to tell—Mr. Lyons had been breathing fire!

The waiter no longer attempted to smile. His dinner service was ruined. He removed the firepot with the soup bowls and poured wine all around. They would just have to wait for the Mandarin duck, he thought with an affronted sniff.

A light eater, Roxie didn't know how much longer she could handle these elaborate dinners. Because she had gone to the Plum Blossom with Rusty on Saturday night, Julian insisted that she now owed him an evening. He had begged so nicely that she just couldn't say no, and now she found herself being ushered into the Pyramid Room of the Fairmont Hotel for continental cuisine.

The French maître d' snapped his fingers for waiters and a sommelier. Roxie would have felt claustrophobic had they not kept a discreet distance, never swarming or fawning but instantly available at the slightest glance. Julian ordered the finest wine on the menu, and when he had approved it, the sommelier poured, first for Roxie, then for Julian.

"To the most beautiful woman in Dallas," Julian said, lifting his glass to Roxie. "And the smartest businesswoman."

"Why, Julian, how sweet," she murmured, giving him her best smile. She sipped the wine, savoring its bouquet, while the waiter prepared their Caesar salad at a cart beside the table. With deft precision he stirred and blended, then presented his beautiful creation to Roxie.

"Madame," he said, bowing.

"Umm, this is delicious," she murmured.

"Only a starter," Julian replied. "Wait until you taste the pheasant. It's baked in a clay pot with a crust. Absolutely divine!"

They talked quietly while they ate their first course, and Julian appreciated Roxie with his eyes. She looked so beautiful, her eyes bright and sparkling, her color vibrant. She wore a dress with long, full sleeves and a full skirt made of a rust-colored taffeta that swished when she moved. How unusual that a woman so beautiful had such a good head for business, Julian thought. He glowed as he contemplated the empire they could build with their combined ability and her father's capital.

Roxie looked around the sophisticated restaurant with its heavy, starched linen tablecloths, its leather-lined walls, to the important Dallasites who were dining nearby. A four-star restaurant much favored by the rich and powerful, tonight the Pyramid Room had a full complement of guests whose pictures were in the Dallas *Morning News* at least once a week. Three oil barons were at an unobtrusive corner table, a group of prominent bankers at another. A famous federal judge was receiving superior service at the table he shared with the president of the American Bar Association. And everywhere there were gorgeous women in high-fashion clothes.

"Isn't that Victoria Principal?" she asked, gesturing to a table where there was a small furor of activity.

"Could be. She comes to Dallas a lot."

"I think I saw that dress in Neiman's the other day," Roxie said, admiring a hand-painted silk crêpe de chine blouson gown designed by Michael Katz. She sighed. She loved to go to places where women wore beautiful clothes and important business was transacted in quiet dignity. Her father was rich, but there were so many rich people in Dallas that he'd never achieved the first rank of power and influence which he and Roxie so desired. She turned to Julian with an appraising eye. Julian had a fantastic head for business, and he, too, loved the finer things of life. She visualized him in a tuxedo at the Dallas Country Club, herself in a show-stopping ballgown, as they presided over the major charity function of the year. She gave him an adoring smile.

"Never mind, waiter, we'll just join our friends at this table," said a robust voice.

"Oh, no, not again!" Roxie cried in dismay. "Dad, you can't be eating at the Pyramid Room! You know this rich food is bad for you."

But her words fell on deaf ears. George, accompanied by Lorraine this time, insisted that the waiter seat them with his "baby girl" and her date. The waiter, imperturbable, murmured, "No problem," and almost by magic two additional plates were set for the newcomers. Before George and Lorraine could turn in their order for the rack of lamb, there was another slight disruption as Rusty and Karla O'Connor, Julian's secretary, joined them. The waiter took Rusty's order for beef Chauteaubriand, and Julian ordered two more bottles of very expensive wine. They were going to need it.

"Dad, this spying has got to stop!" Roxie scolded at work the next day.

"Now, Roxie, you can't blame us men for being curious and wanting to keep track of who's ahead in the contest." He had been afraid that last night's shenanigans had tried Roxie's limited patience—and sure enough, she had burst into his office like a German rocket the first thing this morning.

"Dad, I want to get to know these men better so I won't have to marry a stranger in six months. And how do you expect me to get to know them if I never get to be alone with them? Just about the time we're starting to have a real talk, here come four extra people!"

George urged her to sit down on the couch and quickly brought her a cup of steaming black coffee. "Lorraine," he called into the intercom, "will you see if you can find something out there for Roxie to eat? She's hungry and it's put her in a bad mood."

"Daddy," Roxie sputtered in anger, "I am *not* hungry. As a matter of fact, I'm fed up—to here," she cried, gesturing in the general vicinity of her chin.

"Now, Roxie, don't be mad at your old dad. I just have your best interests at heart, that's all."

"How can you say that, when I'll never have the nerve to set foot in the Pyramid Room again—or the Plum Blossom, either, after you created all that confusion." She took a sip of the coffee, then had to wait to swallow until it quit scalding her mouth.

"Well, you see, sweetheart, I just want to be sure the best man gets you in six months. Thought I ought to keep an eye on things and see that everything was all above-board. Everything fair and square and all that, you know." George squirmed uncomfortably. How could he tell her that he really just wanted to be part of something fun and adventuresome? Life had gotten dull for him the past few years, and this contest idea of Roxie's had perked him up more than a high-rolling business deal. Life might be passing him by, and he wasn't one of the dragon-slayers any more—but did that mean he didn't even get to watch the young knights joust? No, that would be too cruel. He sneaked a peek at Roxie, whose hands were fidgeting restlessly in her lap. Was there any way to explain to her how the old king feels when new warriors are doing battle to take his place?

"Dad, all we were doing was having dinner. Do you mean you thought I might be plotting with one of those men to tilt the contest in his favor?"

George nodded. It wasn't true, but it sounded like an excuse she would believe.

"That's crazy. Why would I do a thing like that? It doesn't make any difference to me which one of them wins. I've decided either one of them will do just fine." She thought again of a life with Rusty and scads of money in the bank, or life with Julian and a slot in the ruling class. Yes, either one would be just fine!

"Oh, I didn't really think *you* would do anything like that," George said, quickly retracting his lie. "But you never know what one of these VP's might try. They've both worked for me a long time, you know, and I'm onto their tricks. Their motto is 'Winning is Everything.'"

"Isn't that the kind of man you want for a son-in-law? It's certainly the kind of man I want for a husband." Roxie's chin set in a stubborn line.

Lorraine came in the room with an orange and a hard-boiled egg. "Sorry to interrupt," she said, "but here's a bite for you to eat."

"Lorraine, this is your lunch!" Roxie cried, refusing the food.

"Oh, I don't need any lunch today. That lamb with the mint jelly last night was quite filling, not to mention the chocolate soufflé. I'm going to have to diet for a week." She turned to her boss with a gentle smile. "But I certainly do thank you for taking me to such a nice place. I've never eaten at the Pyramid Room before, though I've heard about it for years."

"Well, then," George beamed, "we'll just have to try it again sometime. Your company was delightful, just delightful."

"Dad," warned Roxie.

"Oh, just the two of us, of course. Roxie's been chewing on me all morning for interrupting her date. Says I'm not allowed to join her in the future." George's lips turned down in self-pity. He was just an old dog, relegated to the back porch while the puppies got to frisk in the living room. What was he going to do with himself in six months, when Roxie was married? "Shoo, shoo, you women run on and let me get my work done."

"Roxie, I think you hurt your dad's feelings," Lorraine said as they walked down the plush-carpeted hallway toward their own offices.

"Oh, no, I'm sure I didn't," Roxie objected, reaching into Lorraine's out basket for the letters which had already been typed. "These look fine. Let me borrow a pen and I'll sign them now, then you can put them in the early mail."

"I've never seen him look so depressed," Lorraine insisted as she handed over a felt marker pen for Roxie's hastily scrawled signature.

"Oh, Lorraine, you worry too much. Besides, Dad needed a good piece of my mind. I was never so embarrassed in all my life. Why, our table in the restaurant was worse than O'Hare field in a blizzard."

"Your dad was just curious and wanted to see who had the head start in the contest."

"Nobody has a head start—I'd say it was a dead heat at this point." She handed the letters to Lorraine and tossed the pen back onto the desk. "At least as far as Rusty and Julian are concerned. I suppose Todd Kendrick doesn't even know the race has started, the creep. I doubt if he'll ever leave the starting line."

"What makes you say that?" Lorraine briskly folded the letters and inserted them in their envelopes, then tossed them in the outgoing mail.

Roxie reached for the stack of phone messages that had accumulated while she was in her father's office. It looked like the contest had set off a burst of business activity, with calls coming in from all over the country in regard to various real estate development projects.

"Umm, this looks interesting," she said. "I'll return this call first. Maybe I'll get a free trip to Acapulco to look at a resort location."

"Roxie, you didn't answer my question."

Roxie looked up with a lifted eyebrow. "What question?"

"What makes you so sure that Todd Kendrick is going to lose the contest?"

"Well, of course he's going to lose the contest." In irritation Roxie jerked her mauve angora sweater down over a darker mauve tweed skirt. "You can tell by his division's financial statements that the guy's nothing but a loser."

Lorraine laughed. "Maybe you better look back at some of last year's financial statements. Todd has been known as a boy wonder ever since he came to work for your dad. I think one month his profits were more than Rusty's and Julian's put together."

Roxie looked up in momentary interest, then shrugged off the information. "Apparently King Midas lost his touch. Thank goodness," she added sarcastically. "Can you think of anything worse than having to marry a Grim Reaper like him? I don't think he even shaves more than once a week. And his clothes look like he's just pulled them out of the bottom of the clothes hamper."

"Why, Roxie, how unkind!" Lorraine clicked her tongue in disappointment.

"Now, Lorraine, don't tell me you're going to stick up for him. A guy like that, with a perpetual frown on his face?" Roxie tugged at her sweater again and started back to her own office.

"He's going through a bad time right now," Lorraine said sympathetically. "He never used to be like this. In fact, the secretaries used to fight to do his work. He was quite a lady killer. Not that *he* did anything improper," she quickly added. "He was unusually considerate, as a matter of fact. Women just seemed to be swept away by his golden good looks and that sexy smile."

"I find that very hard to believe," Roxie retorted, her slim hips swaying as she hurried to her office. From the doorway her voice echoed, "Frankly, Lorraine, I think Todd Kendrick is nothing but a grouch."

"Is that so?" demanded an angry voice from near the window.

Startled, Roxie looked up to see Todd Kendrick himself standing inside the room. "What are you doing in my office?" she snapped.

"Waiting for you to finish gossiping about the hired help," he replied, his words chilled with arrogance.

His piercing brown eyes raked her casual skirt and sweater, and he passed a hand through his wheat-colored hair. A flush darkened his face, accenting the strong chin and handsome features. For a moment he considered straightening the knot in his tie, then stubbornly left it askew. "As long as we're trading insults, that purple color looks awful on you."

"It isn't purple, it's *mauve,* and *I* happen to like it."

"Suit yourself, if you want to look like a middle-aged matron at a bridge party." He walked toward her and sat down with an insolent slouch on one of the white chairs that contrasted with the jade green carpeting in her office. He leaned back and folded one long leg over the other, rudely ignoring the fact that it was her office and she was still standing.

"Boy, do you ever have a nerve!" she said, anger overriding her discomfiture. "Why don't you just tell me what you've come for and then leave? I have a lot of work to do today." She marched past him and lowered her tiny frame into the chair behind her desk, her shoulders squared, her chin high in an attempt to seize control of the situation.

Todd rubbed his finger along his jaw. "As a matter of fact, I shaved this morning. Would you like to check?" He started to rise.

"That isn't necessary," she protested, anger making her voice sharp. She gritted her teeth. "Just tell me what you came for and get out."

"Of course, your highness." He tossed a folder onto her desk. "Just sign off on that contract and I'll be on my way."

Roxie opened the folder and scanned a proposal for a high-rise luxury hotel on the Florida coast near

Pensacola. "Where did this project come from? We've never discussed a Florida beach project in our planning meetings."

"No, we haven't. But western Florida is on the verge of a boom. There are miles of sandy beaches as white as the Caribbean that haven't been touched by developers. This is a chance to get in before prices skyrocket."

Roxie leaned back in her chair and gave the documents closer scrutiny. The proposal seemed to be carefully assembled, with an abundance of supporting data. She found that any question which occurred to her had been anticipated by the person who prepared the proposal, with well-researched answers already set out for her in the documentation.

"This is very interesting," she said, looking up to find Todd's eyes fixed upon her. "Who prepared this proposal?"

"Why, I did, of course. Glad you like it." His sarcastic tone irritated Roxie.

"I didn't say I liked it," she answered. "I said it was interesting." Was the man so conceited that he thought he could burst in here and overwhelm her in nothing flat with a new idea? "How long have you known this piece of beach front property was available?"

For a moment Todd just glowered at her and refused to answer. "What difference does that make?"

"Because land prices change fast. You may not be able to get it at this price now."

"Oh, I can get it, all right. I took an option on it six months ago, and the option is still good."

"You took an option on a million dollar property and then let it sit for six months?" Roxie was horrified. That went against the grain of everything she had been taught in her MBA program and at the Chicago bank. "How much interest have you had to pay while the option lay dormant?"

Todd's eyes narrowed dangerously. She was much too close to a raw nerve. Six months ago, only days after he had taken this option, his wife left him for another man and his life had caved in. What did he care about a stupid option when it had taken all his grit just to live from one day to the next, so badly had he been hurt? What would this spoiled little princess know of broken hearts and shattered dreams? She lived in a gold-plated world where the only thing that counted was money.

"Look," he said angrily, "the losses have already been charged to my division. Now do you want to let me recoup them or not?" He rose in his chair and held out his hand to take the file from her.

Roxie waved him back into his seat. "Just hold your horses. I said I was interested."

"Don't be high-handed with me," he warned. "I might put up with that from your father because I respect him and he's getting old. But I'm not about to sit here and let you get away with the same tactics."

"Is that because I don't have the excuse of being old?" she asked sarcastically. His previous words still vibrated in the air. "Or is it because you don't respect me?"

"Why don't you figure that out for yourself? It ought to be easy enough for a smart cookie like you."

They glared at each other, Roxie's blue eyes hurling

darts of flame into his brown ones, only to have them deflected and hurled back at her. Anger bounced around them like bolts of electricity, sizzling in the air.

The intercom buzzed. "Roxie, your dad wants you to stop by his office on your way to lunch. He says Todd Kendrick left a proposal on his desk this morning that really looks fantastic and he wants to see what you think of it."

Roxie shook her head in disgust. "Tell him I'll stop by in about an hour."

After a short pause during which Lorraine relayed this information to George Lyons, her voice came back over the intercom. "Sorry, he changed his mind. He said for you to have lunch with him and he'll get Todd to come along to explain it in person."

"No. Tell him I have other plans for lunch." She turned back to Todd. "Leave the proposal with me for now. I'll study it some more and talk to Dad about it later." She rose.

Todd stood, his pride stung at being dismissed as though he were a person of no consequence. "What's the matter, your highness?" he said. "You don't care to eat with commoners?"

"Your manners are certainly common," she replied icily. "And frankly, I think your proposal would do better to speak for itself—until such time as it acquires a persuasive spokesman."

He crossed the space between them in two steps. "And what kind of persuasion would a woman like you understand?" he said angrily, grabbing her shoulders. "Your mind is too small to comprehend anything except money." His breath was warm against her face, and she jerked away from him. "Well, that's just fine," he added. "This Florida project will make the company a fortune. Even someone with your superficial values can see that!" His voice fell as he stepped away from her with a look of disdain. "You just go right ahead and study this proposal. You take all the time you want. But then you're going to come running to me to carry it out, because nobody else in the company can put together a complicated deal like this one—including you!" He turned on his heel and stormed out of the room.

Chapter Three

$\mathcal{R}$oxie hurried down the wrought-iron spiral staircase to her living room below, fastening a fresh-water pearl earring as she did so. She had decided to keep her jewelry simple so that nothing would detract from the spectacular effect of her white linen pajama outfit, lavished with wide bands of cutout Battenberg lace at the hem, yoke and cuffs. The same heavy lace was scrolled across the front of the trousers from the wide hems to her hips. She had rolled her hair on a hundred tiny rollers, then brushed it into a halo of tangled curls. Shimmering eyeshadow emphasized the sparkle in her eyes, and an artist's palette of colors, expertly applied, highlighted the contours of her face.

"Dad, I'm so glad you're early," she cried, giving him a warm hug. "Look around, will you, and see if I've forgotten anything? The caterer is already in the kitchen working on the appetizers, and the bartender should be here any minute."

"Now, now, don't rush me," George grumbled good-naturedly. "Let me get a look at you first."

Roxie lifted a graceful arm and twirled several times, just as she had done as a little girl. "Will I do?"

George's heart filled with pride. His baby girl was a beauty, all right, and what's more, she knew how to make the most of her looks. Why, not even one of those fancy New York models could look any better than his Roxie. "Oh, you look just gorgeous, princess. What do you call those pants things you've got on?"

"Hostess pajamas. Aren't they cunning?"

"Pajamas—to sleep in?" The terminology was lost on George.

"No, Daddy," Roxie giggled. "Not at $950 a pair. Now will you please make a quick inspection for me? I get so excited before a party that I wouldn't notice something drastic. I'm always afraid I'll leave my pantyhose drying on the shower rod in the bathroom!"

"I'll check the bathroom first, but I'm going to hurry so I can see what's going on in the kitchen. Something in there sure smells good." He started toward the staircase to take a quick look at Roxie's bedroom upstairs, knowing from past experience that he'd find some strewn clothing that she had overlooked.

"The caterer is making fried cheese balls. Tell her to let you have a taste. I'll be in the dining room checking the silverware."

This was her first party since she had been back in

Dallas, the first large-scale entertaining she had done on her own, and she wanted everything to be perfect. She had invited all the officers of Sunshine Enterprises, of course, and many of their major clients. There were even some friends from the bank in Chicago who had promised to fly down, hoping to pick up another commercial account or two. A few friends from high school days at the Hockaday School for Girls were coming—with their husbands—and even a few old boyfriends from St. Mark's. Her restless fingers needlessly rearranged a few sprigs of greenery in the centerpiece, and she decided it had been worth the expense to fly in Oriental poppies from California. Their bright orange was a sophisticated contrast to the white plush carpeting and teal blue upholstery of the chairs.

Some of the food was already on the table, each item in a coordinated serving piece. There were plenty of napkins, and the catering staff would promptly wash up dirty plates so that her supply of Wedgewood would be adequate. She quickly checked the wet bar and found plenty of ice, liquor and glasses. Everything was ready. There was nothing left to do but wait for her guests to arrive and let the party happen.

She walked back across the living room and opened the French doors out onto the terrace. It was a small terrace, since her townhouse on Turtle Creek had a minuscule lot, but she had dozens of potted trees and roses that created the effect of a garden. The roses wouldn't bloom for a few more weeks, but already buds had formed and were hidden in the new green leaves. Roxie sat down on a patio chair and sighed with happiness.

"Have a bite," George mumbled as he joined her, his mouth full of caviar on toast. "Looks like you've planned quite a party."

"Later. I'm too excited to eat right now."

"Having fun?"

"Oh, you bet. I haven't given a party since I left Chicago. It's going to be great to see my old friends. Besides, I think we'll do some business, too. I asked the clients that I thought would be vulnerable to my . . . ah, blandishments, in a more informal setting." She giggled.

"Roxie, don't you ever think about anything but business?" Her father gave her a piercing look. She had been gone for such a long time, five years in Chicago, four years before that to Stanford University. He was beginning to think he really didn't know his own daughter very well. Ninety-fifth percentile in aggressiveness and ambition, zero in personal relations, and she was only twenty-seven years old! What was the world coming to?

"Well, of course I think about other things besides business. I think about clothes, and parties, and traveling, and jewelry—all the important things! And men, lately—since this contest has been on my mind. But mostly," she admitted with a twinkle, "I think about business. Because it comes first, before you can buy the other things that make life so wonderful." She leaned back and stretched, pleased with herself and pleased with life.

"What about the contest? My phone has been

ringing off the wall since those VP's got off their duffs and got to work. That Florida proposal of Todd Kendrick's is really something. Rusty and Julian are going to have to build a fire in the engine to catch up."

"Oh, pooh. It may be a good idea, but Todd doesn't have the gumption to bring it off. I imagine I'll end up doing the work on that one," she said disdainfully.

"What do you mean? You can't just step in and take over somebody else's project, Roxie. Todd would never forgive you—and neither would I—if you undercut him that way."

"Oh, I won't have to undercut him. He's in over his head, and pretty soon he'll be begging for my help."

Even to the father who loved her so dearly she sounded smug. "Roxie, why do you insist on downgrading Todd? He's a very bright guy—a creative genius, actually. He can look at a piece of land and see possibilities for developing it that no one else would even think of."

Roxie stood up and paced the terrace in irritation. "What is it about that guy that makes everybody defend him? He's a jerk, a loser, moping around feeling sorry for himself because his wife dumped him. Well, I for one don't blame her! I just don't understand why she didn't do it *sooner.*"

"This isn't like you, Roxie. You always get along with everybody, especially men—always have. Yet you don't even give Todd a chance, just write him off, when you don't even know him."

"I know him as well as I want to, thank you very much. He's rude, he's arrogant, he's self-righteous—" She sputtered to a stop, unable to think of enough scathing adjectives to do the man justice.

George leaned back and pondered this stranger who was his daughter. "Careful, Roxie," he said gently. "You don't want to say things you may regret. Words like that can stick in your craw if you have to eat them later."

"Well, you certainly don't need to expect me to change my mind about Mr. Kendrick. You and Lorraine may be taken in by him—but frankly, Dad, I charge that up to senility." Before George could make an indignant response, she smiled and changed the subject. "Come on," she said, "let's go stir up something to drink. This will be my last chance before the evening's over."

Within the hour Roxie's townhouse was filled with the sound of people laughing and talking, of ice tinkling in never-empty glasses. The first guests arrived in a solid stream, so she had to stay at the door to greet them; but later she was able to mix with the crowd, hurrying back to the door when the bell rang. She had invited a good mix of age groups and occupations so every guest could find someone interesting to talk to. She caught snatches of conversation on every topic from personal computers and physical fitness to modern art and local politics. Her party was a hit, and she was thrilled.

At the mid-point of the evening she hurried to answer the bell and found Todd Kendrick at her doorstep. "Well, my goodness," she said, summoning her best hostess smile, "this is a surprise." Drat him, she thought angrily. Why did he come? She'd had to invite him, since she'd invited all the other Sunshine Enterprises VP's. But didn't he know the difference between a genuine invitation and one which was purely *pro forma?*

His smile was equally artificial, his eyes cold. "Observe," he said, drawing her eyes to his clothing. "No wrinkles."

Her eyes skimmed lightly down his body. He wore a pair of dark brown slacks with a camel's hair blazer over a heather-toned sweater, its V-neck exposing an immaculate shirt collar. His dark loafers had either been given a frenzied spit polish or were brand new. He looked pretty damn good, but she would die before she admitted it.

"Congratulations," she said testily. "I see you've finally had your laundry done."

His brown eyes narrowed to a slit. "And shaved, too. After all, this is a command performance. Wouldn't do to insult royalty, now would it?"

Roxie's plastered-on smile disintegrated. Social amenities were completely wasted on this boor. "Look, Kendrick, there's no point in going through the motions. I don't like you and you don't like me. Let's just leave it at that."

He put his arms against the doorpost at either side of her head, imprisoning her, then lowered his head until their faces were scant inches apart. "Why, my dear Roxanne, how can you say that?" he asked, his words carrying all the warmth of a snow cone in December. "I'm madly in love with you, can't you see that? In six months we'll be married."

She twisted her head to one side, looking for an ally among her guests to rescue her. But everybody was involved in a conversation, and even if anyone had noticed her, he would have assumed from their compromising posture that she was carrying on another of her famous flirtations. She would have to defend herself.

"Over my dead body!" she retorted angrily. "You'll *never* win the contest, you—you—you third-rate stooge!"

His big hand clamped over her chin, forcing her eyes to meet his. For an unguarded moment she saw something raw and vulnerable in his eyes, but then a curtain fell, hiding his pain. "You're going to retract those words," he insisted.

Her dander was up now, and she set her chin in a stubborn line, vigorously shaking her head. His fingers caught in her tousled curls and yanked, none too gently.

"Ouch!" she cried.

"Take it back," he demanded. His chin was set in the same stubborn line as her own.

There was a silent, intense war of wills as his body pressed her back against the doorpost. He wasn't unusually tall but was nicely proportioned, lean and long-legged with broad shoulders and well-developed biceps. The top of Roxie's head grazed his collarbone, and she felt the angry hammer of his heart against her cheek, the warm rasp of his breath against her hair. His body had a surprising strength against hers, the muscles firm and hard—quite unlike the usual male office-worker, she thought idly as she dug her heels into the floor and resisted him physically and mentally without having to take a single step away.

"I'll take it back when you prove me wrong," she said at last, realizing that their physical stance was open to misinterpretation by her guests.

"I'll prove you wrong and get that retraction," he said, a vein throbbing in his temple. "I'll win the damned contest and make you rue the day you underestimated my ability." He loosened his grip and Roxie moved away from him with a shaky breath. "You don't mind if I have a drink, as long as I'm here? Always had a hankering to mix with royalty," he added with a rude snort.

"Hey, Todd, there you are," called George Lyons, hurrying across the room to join them. "Wondered where you were, son. Glad you could make it."

Roxie's hostess smile was back in place, though it had slipped just a trifle. "Yes, so glad you could make it," she lied. "Daddy, won't you take Todd to the bar? He said he was dying for a good stiff drink." Her dignity intact even if her pride had been rudely assaulted, she turned in a movement almost regal, head high and shoulders squared, to join a nearby group of friends. Her angry tears would have to wait.

For the remainder of the party Roxie was even more animated and vivacious than before. Perhaps her cheeks were a little bright, but since her tawny skin was given to vibrant coloring anyway, nobody suspected that it was anything other than the radiance of good health. She wandered to a group where Hamlin Ayres stood with his new fiancée, Sybil Forrester, and extended her congratulations. A mocking voice inside Roxie's head inquired whether she would have had to endure Todd Kendrick's insults if Ayres were a contender in the race. Probably it didn't matter. Something had put a burr under Kendrick's saddle to get him rared up and ornery, and with or without Ayres in the contest, Kendrick was going to be a mean son-of-a-gun. She kept her distance and watched warily out of the corner of her eye.

Odd, though, that his anger had had such a devastating effect on her. A lifetime with a father whose temper had the world's shortest fuse had given her ample experience with irascible men, and usually she was an expert at defusing and soothing ruffled feelings. Yet something about Todd's anger had invaded her very being, toppling her defenses, and she had experienced it as though it were her own emotion. If only she hadn't caught that brief, unguarded, awful revelation of his pain. Why didn't he have more self-respect than to expose his vulnerability to her that way?

She felt a piercing discomfort, as though she had intruded on the most private chambers of his being and unearthed a carefully guarded personal secret. It was a secret that imposed a heavy responsibility, one she was unwilling to be burdened with. She had never allowed herself to know another person except in a carefully structured social role, nor had she allowed anyone else to know her except in the same way. She wanted the safety of superficial relationships that asked for and gave up nothing.

She flitted from group to group, constantly aware that Todd was never far away. She was astonished to find that he quickly became the center of a lively group and that he had caught the attention of her longtime friend Marc Stanley, a prominent young Dallas attorney. They left the group for a quiet corner and had a heavy discussion which had all the earmarks of a high-dollar business deal. The nerve of you, Todd Kendrick, she thought, to use *my* party, and *my* friend, for *your* business deal.

She huffily turned her back and joined Julian Mackley and Rusty Wales. "Having fun, guys?" she asked with a bright smile. They looked up guiltily as though they had been caught reading dirty books under the covers with a flashlight.

"Oh, sure, great party, Roxie," Rusty said with enthusiasm, and hurriedly began talking about the excellent smoked salmon in an effort to change the subject.

"What's going on over here?" she asked. "You two have had your heads together all evening. It's not like you to be so quiet."

Neither man wanted to answer the question, and both squirmed, hoping the other would find something to say. An attempt to talk about the local City Council elections failed miserably, and Roxie's intuition warned her that Julian and Rusty were up to no good.

"All right, fellows, out with it. Have you robbed the company cookie jar or what?"

The false accusation startled the truth out of Rusty. "Never!" he said in a horrified whisper. "We've just put our heads together to come up with something that will make more money than that new project of Todd's. We never expected him to offer any competition—and now he's the *front runner*."

"You mean you're working together to beat him?" Roxie was confused. "This isn't a team competition, you know."

Julian laughed silkily. "No, but we need to join forces for the moment to outdistance Todd. Then we'll go back to competing with each other."

Roxie smiled. This sounded interesting. "What do you have in mind?" she asked so sweetly that they couldn't refuse to answer. "Maybe I can help."

Roxie slipped out onto the patio to pull together her confused thoughts. The party was at the point where it could run itself without her, and she needed a breath of cool air and a moment's solitude. She wandered over to one of the redwood planters and toyed with a stem on a rosebush, her eyes gazing at the midnight sky with its myriad twinkling stars, almost close enough to touch.

"Following me?" inquired an arrogant voice.

"Ouch," she said, pricking her finger and instinctively sticking it into her mouth. Todd Kendrick stood less than two feet away from her, and she quickly turned to leave. "Sorry, I didn't realize you were out here. I'll leave you to your privacy."

He shrugged indifferently. "Guess there's enough sky for both of us."

"It's beautiful, isn't it?" she answered with forced politeness, determined to perform her hostess role adequately. "I missed the Texas sky during those years I was away. I don't think the stars are as bright anywhere else as they are here."

The darkness wrapped them in a kind of intimacy that Roxie found threatening, and she turned to leave, her sandal heels clicking on the terrazzo floor. She brushed past Todd, closely enough that he caught the scent of her perfume. "You're wearing that same perfume," he said almost against his will, with a strange, unexpected lurching in his gut. "What is it?"

"Diorissimo. It's my favorite. I always wear it."

"It's nice." There was a strained silence, and in the starlight they felt the throbbing of the universe echo in their own heartbeats. "Look," he said on a strange impulse, "I didn't mean to be rude to you earlier. Not that it's any excuse, but I haven't been myself lately. I shouldn't have taken my bad mood out on you."

"Don't worry about it," she said, hoping that he would drop the subject. She really didn't want to discuss that earlier conversation or think about its effect upon her. "I'm used to hot-tempered men."

"Yeah . . . Well, I've had my turn out here. I'll go inside and let you have yours."

"No, really, you stay. I need to go back in and check on the party anyway."

Todd gave a sardonic laugh. "We're an odd pair. Either we're exchanging insults or exchanging courtesies. There ought to be a middle ground."

"What do you mean, 'middle ground'?"

He reflected a moment. "Oh, where we wouldn't show only our best or our worst side, but the way we really are."

Her next words slipped out involuntarily before Roxie could censor them. "My goodness, you expect a lot from people, don't you?" As soon as she asked the question, she knew that she had made a terrible mistake and invited the very subject which she wanted to avoid.

"Of course. Don't you?"

"I expect people to do their jobs," she answered curtly. "I don't ask anything else except that they be civil."

"In other words, you prefer superficial politeness?"

"Absolutely. Don't you? I mean, our disagreements with one another really don't bear repetition, wouldn't you agree?"

He leaned back against the cool brick and studied her face in the starlight. "I'm not sure. At least when you're insulting me I know there's a real person inside that beautiful packaging of yours."

"Oh, come on," she protested.

"No, I mean it. There you are, gorgeous clothes, gorgeous makeup, gorgeous hair—but you're like some beautiful china doll. Where's the real woman underneath all that tinsel and glamour?"

She turned away, her eyes downcast. "Who knows?" she said brightly in an effort to deflect his searching questions with charm. "Maybe I'm just one of those fancy-wrapped Christmas packages with nothing inside."

"I've been wondering who you really are," he answered. "In fact, it's about the only thing that's caught my attention since . . . my divorce."

This had gone entirely too far. She had to get away from him and get back to the safety of the crowd. "You must excuse me," she said. "There's a whole house full of people, and I've been shirking my duties as hostess."

She tried to move inside, but his arms slipped around her, so naturally it seemed that they belonged there, and pulled her close against him. His big hands, tender in their strength, moved up her back, stroking and caressing her, then lost themselves in the abandon of her curly hair.

"Roxie, don't go yet," he said softly.

She pressed her face against his chest. What should she do? It was wonderful to be held in his arms, to feel his heart pounding against hers, the brush of his lips against her hair. And yet . . . something warned her that if he kissed her, it would be no ordinary kiss, that it would give too much, demand too much.

"Roxie." His hand found her chin and tilted her face upward. "You're so tiny," he whispered. "Just a wisp of a thing." His hands found her waist. "You see," he said, "I can span your waist with my hands. And yet you keep everybody at a distance with that strong will of yours."

He stood in the April moonlight and waited, as though there were all the time in the world. But while he waited, he held her close, his hands around her face, his thumbs stroking the contours of her cheekbones. And while he held her, he gazed into her eyes, holding back nothing of himself, and let her read for herself his pain, his anger, his disillusionment.

She shook her head. "You scare me," she said. "You expect too much." She pressed her arms against his chest to separate their bodies, her hands resting lightly on his shoulders.

"I won't take more than you want to give," he said softly, his fingers toying with her hair. He turned his head slightly and brushed his lips against her hand. When his eyes met hers again, a twisted smile mingled with his pain.

Butterflies went topsy-turvy in her stomach. She

had the feeling that she was about to take a running leap into space and might wake up on another planet. But the fear was giving way to a desire to know. Who was she, anyway, besides being Daddy's girl and a tough businesswoman? She lifted her face. It was time she found out.

His head moved toward her in slow motion, his cheek brushing hers. And then their lips met in a shy, hesitant, introduction that lasted only an instant, as though he wanted to say, "It's not too late, you can still change your mind." But when she stayed within the safe circle of his arms and slid her own arms around his neck, his head lowered again. Now his lips were searching, gentle still, but exploring hers with delicious pressure, salty and tingling. His arms tightened around her, pulling her body closer against his until she could feel the contours of his desire. She stood on tiptoes, luxuriating in the tautness of her body against his, the pressure of her breasts against his chest.

His lips moved across her cheek to her eyelids, down to her ear, against her thick hair, then settled in the hollow of her neck until his eager nibblings sent desire coursing through her. She felt the ripple of his shoulder muscles underneath his jacket and stroked the scratchy wool fabric with fingers that had an eager life of their own. Her mind, recently so staunch against him, was overcome by the sheer magnetism of his nearness, and she found herself wondering how his bare skin would feel against her own.

Todd felt vaguely surprised that his own hostile attitude toward Roxie was dissipating with the heat from his long-quelled physical desire. He felt the caress of her fingers, the tension in her agile body as she strained against him. Could this be the same woman he'd wanted to shake in irritation only an hour earlier? He luxuriated in the feel and smell of her, the tickle of her hair against his cheek. Reckless with wanting, he ached now to hold her tightly and explore the soft curves that yielded against him. With a tremulous sigh Roxie shifted in his arms in an instinctive effort to bring their bodies closer together. "I think the lady is awake," he murmured with an amused laugh. "Now I can give her a real kiss."

Her lips were full and rounded, ripe now for his touch. His mouth caught hers, probing her to a willing response, his teeth nipping at her lip, playful yet persistent. Her lips parted, eager to experience the flavor of Todd's, and their tongues brushed together with sensuous strokes that made her heart race with excitement.

"This is crazy. We don't even—" she whispered brokenly, pulling away from him.

But Todd reached for her again, needing her body to fill the emptiness, and his palms gripped her waist and held her fast while he punctuated his words with hot, demanding kisses. "We don't even what?" he asked in a voice rough with desire.

"We don't even like each other," she answered, trying to evade his questing tongue, though she could not control her trembling response.

His mouth found the sensitive hollow of her neck and aroused it with gentle nips of his teeth. "Maybe we'll learn to like each other once we get better acquainted," he murmured, while his tongue scorched a trail across her collarbone. His fingers slid up her bodice, his thumbs resting on the fabric that covered the peaks of her breasts. Slowly his thumbs began to rotate until he felt her nipples respond, their buds erect and thrusting. "See what I mean?" he said, his lips continuing their lazy search. Impatiently her hands sought the muscled strength of his chest underneath his jacket, even as she felt his hands slip underneath her tunic to explore the soft curves of her hips and breasts. His lips found the secret hollow of her neck, her cheeks, his face warm and scratchy against her sensitive skin.

"Oh, God, Roxie," he whispered urgently, straining against her, pressing her against the brick wall while his hands devoured her. "Please, let me . . ." And then the magic happened. His mouth found hers and claimed it for his own, his tongue igniting hers to a torrid flame and melting her body with a passion she had never known before. The stars of the Texas night exploded.

Chapter Four

Roxie tossed aside the financial projections she'd been working on and left her desk to look again out her rain-spattered window at the traffic below. The monthly executive meeting would start in twenty minutes and there'd still been no word from Todd Kendrick. Where could he be? Daddy would throw a first-class fit if Todd didn't show up. Absenteeism was absolutely not permitted where executive meetings were concerned.

In irritation Roxie yanked the cord to the mini-blinds, snapping them shut against the rain outside, and began to pace the floor. The nerve of Todd Kendrick, anyway, she thought. How dare he melt down her resistance and kiss her with an intimacy she'd never allowed anyone else, then simply disappear without a word? "Damn you, Todd Kendrick. That vulnerability of yours is a contagious disease and I don't want any part of it!" she muttered, feeling angry and entirely too vulnerable.

"Are you talking to me?" called Lorraine from her adjoining office. "I didn't understand what you said."

"I was just thinking out loud," Roxie replied, flopping onto a chair. "Pay no attention." She picked up a well-sharpened pencil and peered intently at the financial data on her desk just in case Lorraine should come in to check on her, but her mind was far, far away.

How was it that Todd Kendrick was able to get under her skin this way? Nobody had been able to distract her mind from business before, not ever. Roxie thought of the dozens of men she'd kissed, with and without passion, always with her every thought and emotion under perfect control. Nothing like this had ever happened to her before, and she didn't like it at all.

It had been over a week since her party, yet she still hadn't been able to erase the memory of Todd's kiss. It came back to haunt her at unexpected moments with a keen, almost poignant, yearning. "Damn you, Kendrick," she whispered softly into the empty room. "I told you you expected too much! We could have kissed, we could even have made love, and then walked away from each other. But no, you wouldn't have it that way! You insisted on getting underneath our masks to the real people underneath. And after you invaded my . . . my privacy, you up and left without a word. I won't have this, do you hear me?"

The silence of the empty room mocked her, and she dropped her head onto her folded arms with a bitter sigh.

"Roxie," called Lorraine from the outer office, "it's time for the meeting. Do you need anything before you go?"

Roxie looked at the diamond-studded watch on her slim wrist and stood, gathering up her notes with a guilty feeling that she wasn't prepared for this executive meeting. But maybe it wouldn't matter. Maybe this time she wouldn't have to carry the ball. Let the other VP's earn their inflated salaries while they tried to win her hand . . . and while she tried to forget that Todd Kendrick had ever been born.

Roxie took her place at the conference table just as her father walked into the room, without time for her usual mild flirtations with the other corporate officers. She noticed an excitement in the room that had been missing in earlier meetings, and Julian and Rusty seemed particularly pleased with themselves. The April financial statement, distributed earlier in the week, showed substantial improvement over the disastrous losses of March, and the room was noisy with congratulations.

"Where's Kendrick?" asked someone down the table from Roxie.

"He'll be along," replied George Lyons. "His secretary said he might be a little late."

Late? For an executive meeting? The other VP's looked at each other with raised eyebrows. Old George's inviolable rule was that everybody had to be on time for these monthly meetings, without exception—yet he seemed unperturbed at Kendrick's absence. Julian sneaked another look at the profit and loss statement and saw that Todd Kendrick's division profits were well below his own. Maybe the old man figured that it didn't matter whether Kendrick was here or not, the way his performance had slipped over the past few months. The old man probably kept Kendrick on the payroll out of sympathy. Julian couldn't help feeling smug as he gazed fondly at his own division's rising profits.

"Let's go ahead and start," said George from the head of the table, shuffling through his folder of papers. "Things are looking up this month. You fellows are doing a great job. Oh, and you, too, Roxie," he added in casual dismissal before turning with a hearty warmth to Hamlin Ayres. "I'm really pleased with your outstanding work this month, Hamlin."

George's smiling comment to a VP whose profits were well below Roxie's own stung her pride. She found herself wondering why her father was so stingy with his praise to her yet generous with other VP's whose accomplishments were less than her own. She began to feel depressed and put on a bright, eager smile to hide her inner feelings.

"Suppose you bring us up to date on the Acapulco project," George said to Julian, and for the next fifteen minutes they heard a careful analysis of a pending real estate acquisition which would, if successful, move Sunshine Enterprises to the forefront of the Mexican tourist industry.

"Excellent work, Julian, absolutely splendid," George said, beaming, when Julian had finished his report. "Now why don't you tell us about this new project you and Rusty dreamed up? I'm sure everybody is eager to hear how the two of you zoomed to first place in the competition for Roxie's hand."

There was a brief flurry as Todd Kendrick entered the room, raincoat tossed over his shoulder and briefcase in one hand. "Sorry, everyone," he murmured and took his seat as quickly as possible. "My plane was late. Go ahead, Julian."

Julian nodded and related a complicated transaction involving the exchange of a rural plot for a piece of prime commercial land. After giving himself full credit for his role in the coup, Julian turned in a sportsmanlike manner to include his teammate. "Rusty really used his supersalesmanship on this deal, because after the owners saw what a nice, quiet place they'd have, they were begging us to move them away from the Six Flags traffic."

Rusty ducked his head and smiled modestly as everybody turned to look at him. "Just fantastic, Rusty," said George, reaching out to pound Rusty's shoulder. "Great teamwork between Marketing and Acquisitions. Proud of you, boys, I'm really proud of you. Now tell us what you have in mind for that little old piece of land there at Six Flags."

"Well, sir," Julian continued, "we've already sold it to one of the luxury hotel chains. Got the sales contract right here. Sunshine Enterprises turned a fantastic profit on that one because we bought low and sold high." Julian and Rusty grinned with pleasure at the hearty congratulations that came their way from the other corporate officers.

"The only problem is that it tied Julian and me in the contest. Our divisions are exactly even this month," Rusty said, sneaking a quick look at his adored Roxie. "What's going to happen if there's a tie?"

"Toss a coin," suggested someone down the table.

"Why, I'll be delighted to marry both of you," Roxie said, turning first to Rusty and then to Julian with a doting smile and a flutter of her lashes. There, take that, Todd Kendrick, she thought, without so much as a glance in his direction.

George chuckled, then turned fondly to Roxie. "Now, boys," he said, reaching over to stroke her cheek. "My baby girl deserves the best. Isn't she the prettiest little thing you ever saw in all your life?"

The men murmured their agreement, and Roxie blushed charmingly, as if on cue, while her gaze flitted around the table. Todd Kendrick leaned back in his chair and watched her for a moment, then turned to survey her effect on the other men in the room. Rusty was practically salivating and the others wore fatuous smiles. "Devastating performance," he said in a low voice.

"What's that?" asked George.

"I said she looks devastating. I have half a mind to win this contest myself."

Julian's disbelieving laugh was more like a bark. "Sure you do."

"We have too big a lead for you to overcome," Rusty said, preening. "Maybe you ought to let Julian and me fight it out." He turned to Roxie with a triumphant smile that made her suspect that he might begin beating his breast Tarzan-style at any moment.

She leaned over and squeezed Rusty's hand, at the same time blowing Julian a kiss. "You know what they say: 'What's good for Sunshine Enterprises is good for Roxie Lyons,'" she said with a glowing smile. In the corner of her eye she caught a glimpse of Todd, shaking his head with a disgusted scowl.

"What will we do if there really is a tie?" asked Julian.

"Now, boys, I told you when we started this contest that the best man would have to win. *Man,* singular. So forget about a tie, because there's only one prize. There has to be a clear winner."

"But—"

"Leave it to me. I'll figure out something if it happens. But it'll be better for profits if you boys heat up the competition and go for a win. Now," he said, turning to Todd, "tell us what you've been up to, disappearing for a whole week without a trace. I couldn't pry any information out of your secretary except that you might be late for the meeting today."

"Don't blame her. She didn't know where I was. Fact is, I didn't know myself until I got there. I flew out to Pensacola and checked out the whole coast, then went around the country visiting hotel chains trying to make a deal on our undeveloped beach property."

"Any luck?"

Todd lowered his head with a frown. "Not yet. The chains will jump on properties in proven tourist areas like Six Flags, but money is so tight they're going slow when it comes to something new. I've got a couple of nibbles, but it may take a while to get it going."

"How long?"

"Maybe six months."

George peered over his glasses at Todd. "The contest will be over by then."

"Yeah, but the Florida coast will be there from now on."

"Nothing you can do to hurry it up?"

"Oh, sure, I suppose. We could go ahead and start a condo project like all that stuff along Padre Island and Port Aransas. But I don't want to develop the new beach that way."

"Why not?" inquired Julian in a haughty voice. "We made a lot of money on the Texas coast."

"And now fourteen college kids in a Jeep can race around on the beach and destroy it. I thought we'd learned something in the past ten years." His chin set in a stubborn line. "Florida doesn't need another Miami Beach."

"Delay costs money," George said, wagging his finger. "We could be turning a profit while you sit there waiting."

"George, in the long run the company will make more money if we wait and do it right. Property values will escalate with proper development. It will be better for the land and better for the company to wait."

"And the contest?" George had to stir Todd's combativeness and keep him in the race. If Julian and Rusty tied for first place, it would be disastrous. Why, they might both quit the company, and then where would he be?

Todd shrugged. "Guess I'll have to find some other way to win." He cast a thoughtful glance in Roxie's direction; she squirmed uneasily, then smiled at Julian.

"Oh, not to worry. I think Rusty and I just about have the contest sewed up," Julian retorted. "I'm sure you haven't seen the April figures, since you've been gone all week, but we're so far ahead of you that you'll be eating our dust for the next five months. You'll never catch up."

"Is that right?" There was neither sarcasm nor scorn in Todd's reply, only the cold steel of self-confidence that made Julian flinch and reminded him of the old days when Todd could waltz him around the table without half trying. Julian took a closer look. Great gods, the guy had shaved.

Roxie, too, took a closer look. Something had happened to Todd. That was plain. He'd never win any awards for cheerfulness, but at least his hang-dog surliness was gone and he had some life to him. He was a damn-sight better looking without that perpetual scowl on his face. Not bad, not bad at all. Her eyes moved from his thick, neatly trimmed hair the color of sun-ripened wheat to his dark golden skin, his strong chin and high cheekbones, that chiseled mouth she'd kissed, so warm and sweet against her own. Her breath caught and it was as though she'd never really seen him before, only looked past him or through him. Her eyes met his and quickly retreated from the dark fires she saw there. He's a brown-eyed blond, she thought in surprise, my favorite combination and I hadn't even noticed. Butterflies fluttered in her stomach, and she fixed her eyes on the April reports, forcing her restless fingers to be still.

George's voice boomed, breaking the tension. "Guess that wraps it up for today, fellows. Time will tell on this contest thing we've got going. Five months is a long time and lots of things can happen. In the meantime, bust your butts!"

The meeting broke up in its usual noisy confusion, with people talking in small groups and rehashing the day's events. Roxie moved from group to group, smiling encouragement to Julian and Rusty until their pulses raced. It was a full ten minutes before Todd was able to catch her alone and pull her aside.

"Sorry I didn't have a chance to call and explain where I was," he said against her ear.

"You certainly don't have to explain your whereabouts to me," she answered, stepping away from the arm at her back. She intended to put a safe distance between herself and the disturbing Mr. Kendrick.

"No, but I thought you might have wondered. You might have expected me to call after—"

"I believe I told you that I don't expect anything from anybody except that they do their job and be civil. You were doing your job—though from the sound of it, you weren't doing it very well."

"Now, just a minute, Lady Bountiful, I thought we'd moved past the insult stage in our relationship."

"What relationship?" she asked, nervousness making her lip tremble. She'd had more than enough of this man. His absence had given her a miserable week, and she'd lost interest in a relationship where she didn't hold all the power. Flirtation was the only way to go. She lifted her head and batted her twinkling sapphire eyes at him.

"Running scared, huh?" he asked, his gold-flecked eyes boring straight through to her soul.

She stood her ground. She'd played Daddy's girl to her father's tantrums long enough to develop expert skills at dissimulation. "Who's scared?" she whispered, running a long painted fingernail down the front of his suitcoat. She straightened his tie, the silk handkerchief in his breast pocket, and smiled enigmatically.

"I've been on the road all week and I'm too tired for your games, Roxie," he said, pushing her hand away. "Let me know when you're ready to talk business."

"I'm always ready to talk business," she said, instantly alert.

"I thought that might get your attention. Let's get out of here." His hand closed on the small of her back and began to push her toward the door.

"Hold it," she said, digging in her heels. "Where are you going?"

"I thought we'd catch a bite to eat and discuss a new project. OK?"

She had no intention of being alone with him in a social situation and was determined to keep their relationship strictly business. "Let's go to my office. I find restaurants too distracting for a serious business talk."

"My God, Roxie, I haven't had anything to eat all day."

"I'm sure Lorraine has something in her desk. She always has cheese and crackers."

"Be reasonable, Roxie. I'm starving."

"What if I send someone out to get you something?"

"Forget it. I'm going home. We can talk about it

tomorrow." His hand fell from her waist, and he took a step away.

She stretched out her hand to stop him. "Why don't you call me at home after you've eaten?"

"No. It's too complicated to talk about over the telephone. I need to show you some sketches so you'll understand what I mean." He paused, waiting for her response.

"What kind of project is it?" Her curiosity was getting the better of her.

"Something we've never done before." He noted the spark of interest in her eyes. "But it'll keep. I'll see you in the morning." He turned to go, sure she would call him back.

She smoothed the furrows in her forehead with a perfectly manicured fingernail. How she loved an innovative project, and Todd might surprise her with a new approach. She'd rather talk business than do anything else. "Todd, wait. Do you promise not to discuss anything except business?"

He gave her a searching look. So she wanted promises that set safe boundaries to keep him from getting too close. Or was it to keep the reins of power in her own hands? Only one way to find out. "I'll take you to the barbecue stand down the street and tell you all about my new idea because I'll need your help to pull it off. But no promises."

She was torn with indecision, but in the end her curiosity and her love of making a deal won the victory. "I'll give you an hour," she said warily, "but that's all. I'll get my raincoat and meet you in the lobby."

* * *

Todd wolfed down two small barbecued beef sandwiches with side orders of pinto beans and potato salad while Roxie sipped a cup of black coffee and toyed with her sandwich. She wasn't about to eat anything so fattening, even though Todd had insisted on ordering it for her. When she got home she'd make a salad and have some fresh fruit. How could Todd eat like that and stay so lean? Her eyes studied him surreptitiously while he polished off the last bite of potato salad. He'd taken off his jacket and loosened his tie, and his crisp white shirt stretched across his shoulders with each motion. He didn't show any signs of flab, nothing but solid muscle.

"Aren't you going to eat your sandwich?" he asked, eyeing it.

"I'm not very hungry."

"Do you mind if I have it, then?"

"Be my guest," she answered, pushing the sandwich in its tissue wrapper across the table. In amazement she watched him devour it in several large bites. "My goodness, where are you putting all that food?"

"I haven't eaten since noon yesterday. I'm famished."

"So I see."

"Did I offend your sense of propriety by asking for your sandwich?" He leaned back with a sigh, his hunger satisfied at last. "I forgot what a high priority you place on civility and the social graces."

"Please," she said with a quick shake of her head. "We didn't come here to debate our personal value systems. Now that you've finished eating, let's get down to business." She was determined to take control of their conversation before he booby-trapped her again.

Todd pushed a hand through layers of golden brown hair, then rubbed his eyes in fatigue. "I guess we'd better," he answered. "Now that I've relaxed, I feel like I've been hit by a ton of bricks. I'm really beat."

"Would you like to wait until tomorrow to talk about this?" Roxie asked, reaching for her purse on the vinyl bench beside her. "No need to push yourself when you're so tired."

Todd waved her back into her seat. "Let me give you something to think about overnight, and we can go over the details tomorrow. You'll need to decide whether to pull some strings for me."

"Me?" Roxie looked up in surprise.

"Here's the plan," Todd answered, opening his briefcase and removing a folder. Beams from the overhead light played on the silky gold hairs at his wrists and knuckles. His well-kept hands flipped through some loose papers, found a group of sketches, and handed them across the table to Roxie.

"What is it?" she asked, looking down at a rough drawing of a golf course with several impressive houses along the fairway.

"You'll have to use your imagination," he said. "I did these sketches myself with a felt marker. Didn't have time to find an artist."

Roxie picked up other sketches, one of several luxurious lodges nestled among pine trees, another of an inn on a bluebonnet-covered hill, another a cluster of cottages surrounding a gallery. In each sketch the buildings seemed to enhance the natural setting, unobtrusive yet beautiful. Roxie lifted her head to find Todd watching her intensely. "I'm intrigued," she said. "Where is it?"

"Right now it's a ranch, almost too scrubby to raise cattle. It's in the Hill Country between Austin and Houston, and the land has a beautiful slope and conformation. I was there this morning, and the bluebonnets were still blooming. I'm itching to see what I can do with it. God, it's loaded with possibilities."

"What do you have in mind?"

"Well, the location makes it ideal. It's close enough for rich people in Houston to have a weekend lodge. And it's also close enough for state politicians who have to keep up a second residence in Austin. It's a little over an hour drive, either way. I think there are enough wealthy people in Houston who'd build a permanent residence if we put in a heliport so they could get back and forth."

Roxie sorted back through the sketches, giving particular attention to the land, and realized that Todd's vision had seen potential that anyone else would have overlooked. She had to give him ungrudging respect and admiration. The guy really had talent. "What else do you have in mind?" she asked.

"I thought we could get Arnold Palmer or Jack Nicklaus or one of the other pros to plan a good eighteen-hole course that would attract wealthy golfers. A tributary of the Colorado River cuts across the ranch, and we could dam it up and have a lake large enough for sailboats. Even build a yacht club. Part of the land could be used for a vacation resort—see the small lodges? There wouldn't be any condos at all on the site. But an inn, with a first-class restaurant, would attract people."

"What's this?" she asked, pointing to the sketch of a gallery.

He grinned. "That's an experiment. You know how every time we try to develop rural properties, we always end up with ramshackle places along the access road? That land is cheap because the rich don't want to live on the outer fringes. I thought maybe we could build some attractive cottages and rent them as studios, make a sort of artists' community for painters, writers, musicians, potters, weavers—whatever. And they could use the gallery to show their work. Don't you think it would give the place a little class?"

"Experiment is the right word, all right." Her forehead furrowed in thought as she tried to visualize the community Todd described. "But it just might work."

"If it goes over at all, it'll go over in a big way," he said with confidence. "Of course, it could also flop in a big way. But I think it's worth the gamble."

"Looks to me like you've got it all figured out. Where do I come into this?"

"You get to pull the strings."

"With Daddy? You don't need me for that. He'll love this whole idea."

"No, not George. With the owner of the ranch. I want you to persuade her to let me develop it."

"Why me?"

"Because she's an old friend of yours from the Hockaday School. Nita Fancher."

"Nita Fancher? Is this her ranch? You've wasted your time, then, because she'll never sell. She doesn't need the money and has an absolute passion for land."

"Then that's why she'll sell. The land is nothing but scrub now, and I can turn it into an oasis for her, give her something to be proud of."

"Why don't you talk to her yourself if you feel that way?"

"I have. I talked to her this morning. But you know how you rich people are, Roxie. You only want to do business with your friends. I know I can persuade her—eventually. But I don't want to lose all that time."

Roxie lifted her eyes to meet Todd's and immediately dropped them again. There was something almost desperate in his expression. Not fear, not worry, but plain old desperation, as though the clock were running out on something vital to him. Curiosity impelled her to ask a loaded question. "This is a big project, Todd. You'll spend years on it. Why does it matter how long it takes to buy the land?"

"Because if we can start quickly enough, I can get part of it designed and financed in time for the profits to count in the contest. And I have to come up with something big, and fast, now that the hotel chains are dragging their feet on the Florida beach property. Otherwise Rusty and Julian are going to walk off with the win."

"Why do you care?" she asked, then waited with tense muscles for him to answer.

He snorted with laughter to conceal his own uneasiness. "Because, dearest Roxanne, I told you I intend to prove you wrong about me."

"You don't have to prove anything to me."

Their glances met and held. This time it was Todd who looked away. He gathered up the sketches and stuffed them back in the folder, then cleared his throat. "I suppose not," he muttered. "Waste of time to try with an uppity female like you."

Roxie looked at her long painted fingernails and briefly contemplated scratching his eyes out. He was rude and exasperating, and she was angry with herself for the gentler feelings she'd had toward him the past hour. She donned her mask, cold and hard, and said in a voice that matched, "Kindly tell me why I should expend any of my energy helping you win the contest. Seems to me I'd wind up with the booby prize if you won."

He gripped her hand until her fingers ached from the pressure. "If Rusty or Julian wins, you'll wind up with a real boob, all right. I'm smarter than both of them put together and I've made more money for your father's company than they'll make in the next twenty years. You're a tough cookie, Roxie, and you always look out for your own self-interest. Open your eyes, lady, and read the writing on the wall. You'll be better off married to someone who can match your brains and ambition instead of someone who'll let you walk all over him." He paused for breath and glared at her across the table. "You're going to help me, Roxie, because deep down inside you want me to win."

Her eyes sizzled with anger, and she wrested her fingers from his grip. "And you're trying to win because deep down inside you want my father's money!"

"You folks about finished?" called the stocky man

in the butcher's apron behind the counter. "It's closing time."

Todd glanced at his watch. "It's seven o'clock. I've used up that hour you gave me. Let's get out of here." He stood and scooped up their dirty paper plates and napkins, then tossed them in a trash container while Roxie started to freshen her lipstick. "Come on," he said. "You're gorgeous enough already."

The rain had stopped while they were in the cafe, leaving the air fresh with the fragrance of the May shower. They walked side by side in the fading dusk, their footsteps echoing on the wet Dallas street, now almost emptied of its commuting office workers. They made no attempt to converse, both still angry with themselves and with each other, and the silence grew strained and awkward.

They approached their darkened parking building, and Roxie would have made her way alone to the ramp where she'd left her Porsche, but Todd insisted on seeing her safely to her car. While she fumbled for her key, he tried to think of an apology that would communicate his regret without accepting blame. It was impossible. He didn't know who was at fault, but they always seemed to get into an argument. Roxie heard his sigh of frustration and looked up in time to catch an enigmatic expression on his face.

"Roxie . . ."

"I know. Forget it. Things will look better tomorrow after we've both had a good night's rest. Next time I'll remember not to discuss business after a hard day at the office."

"Yeah . . . I guess I was too tired and hungry."

She fitted the key in the doorlock and turned it. "Well . . ."

"Yeah . . ." He shifted the briefcase into his other hand so he could open the car door for her.

"Todd . . ."

He looked down at her, one hand resting on her arm. "Yes?"

"Whether or not I help you with Nita Fancher . . . I really like your ideas for the ranch." Something competitive inside Roxie drove her to outperform Todd, yet at the same time she respected his considerable ability. He had more imagination than anybody she'd ever worked with. She gave him a dazzling smile. He deserved it.

The smile hit Todd somewhere below the belt. Despite his resolve to be cautious with Roxie, he felt a sharp throbbing of desire in his groin. He'd told himself a hundred times that he couldn't trust her, yet underneath her tough exterior was something vulnerable and almost shy that intrigued him. And there she was, looking at him with those blue eyes that melted a man's heart and made him forget to protect himself. He dropped the briefcase and pulled Roxie into his arms. "Come here," he whispered, sliding his fingers up her back. "I've got some other ideas I want to share with you."

And then his mouth found hers, warm and moist and so very sweet, as their lips met and clung in an ecstasy of sharing. His tongue urged hers to a joyful exploration that tasted of flesh and nectar, his teeth nipping playfully at her lip until tremors of delight coursed through her. For blissful moments she melted in his arms, awash in a sea of pleasure while she experienced his kisses at her neck and throat, his hands at her breasts and hips. Her fingers crept up his chest and around his neck, drawing him closer into the kiss until their bodies melded together in a cauldron of fire.

It seemed they could no longer breathe, they were so lost in glorious passion. Their hearts hammered together, and Roxie could feel the upsurge of Todd's manhood against her. "Roxie," he whispered, "come home with me."

Slowly she pulled away from him and tried to clear the dazed feeling in her head by drawing in huge, gulping breaths of fresh air. Her foot bumped against something, and she looked down to see his briefcase, abandoned on the concrete floor. His briefcase, containing the plans for the Fancher ranch . . . and he needed her help. Did he think it would be easier to obtain her assistance if he made love to her? It was difficult to think clearly with his hands stroking her body to liquid flame.

"Don't," she said, taking his hand in hers to stop its exquisite torture. "I can't think when you're doing that." She was afraid that Todd might betray her, and she fought against her physical response to him.

"Don't think, Roxie, just feel," he insisted. "Let yourself go, let me . . ." His hand escaped its bondage and sought the softness of her breast, caressing it until it tingled, wanting more. "Please, Roxie, you're so . . ."

"No, Todd, don't," she protested, twisting her body away before it, too, betrayed her.

"Yes . . . you want me, too. Admit it." His mouth

found hers again and demanded entry to its sweet recesses and hollows.

She braced her hands against his chest and pushed. "No, Todd, really. I mean it."

He drew away in disbelief, not comprehending how she could turn off her obvious passion. "What kind of woman are you, anyway? Your body is begging for me to make love to you and that steel-trap mind of yours refuses to give in. What's going on inside that crazy head of yours, anyway?"

He tried again to pull her into his arms, but she stepped out of reach. "I told you before. I'm one of those fancy-wrapped Christmas packages with nothing inside."

His voice was shaking with anger and frustrated desire. "This time I believe you. But I can't figure out how you manage to put out such a hot electric charge when your battery is dead."

He picked up his briefcase and stormed away, leaving her to climb into her car alone. She dropped her head onto the steering wheel and let salty tears run down her cheeks.

Chapter Five

George wandered into Roxie's office and dropped his heavy frame onto one of her chairs. "Have you studied the new financial statement?" he asked, chuckling. "That Julian really built up a good head of steam this past month. I bet Rusty wanted to croak when he saw the figures for May."

Roxie put aside the project she'd been working on to listen to her father's admiring remarks about Julian's ability. "I was a little surprised to see he'd pulled ahead," she responded. "Somehow I'd expected . . ." She paused, then decided to leave the thought unspoken.

"I know, I know," George said, waving his arms as he always did when he was excited. "You thought Rusty would win, since he had the advantage of the Vail ski resort. But I tell you, Roxie, I believe Julian is

going to be able to hold his lead for the next four
months. He's doing wonders in Acapulco.''

Roxie studied the figures on the May report and
tried not to think ahead to September 30th, when the
contest would end. Better to keep her mind on the
present and the intense competition which was raging,
with the lead shifting every week. Business was
booming and she'd never enjoyed her work more than
now, with all the tension and excitement of one big
deal after another. They could hardly keep up with
the paperwork, and she was sure their lawyer would
be able to buy a new Mercedes with his fees from
handling all the real estate transactions. "How is
Todd's Florida project coming along?" she asked.

"Slow, slow," George replied. "I don't think he's
going to be able to get it off the ground in time to do
him any good. Too bad, because he's a nice boy. I like
him. But you'll be just as well off married to Julian.
He's a little flashy, sometimes, but he's ambitious. Or
Rusty, now, he's a good boy, too. But I don't think
he's going to catch up with Julian. They're all fine. I
can't tell you how proud I am of the way they've dug
in and fought to win this contest. I'll say, Roxie, this
was a great idea you had. I'm beginning to wish I had
another daughter to give away!"

Roxie kept her eyes downcast. "Profits have doubled in the past two months, have you noticed?"

"Oh, you bet. Why, I'm busting my buttons over
the way those boys have come through for me. Just
look at Hamlin Ayres's division: He's up 20 percent.
Isn't that grand?"

Roxie's eyes traveled to the right-hand column,
which showed each division's percentage of increase.

Hamlin Ayres was at the bottom with 20 percent, and Roxie's own division was third at 80 percent. Julian was first at 95 percent, Rusty second at 90 percent—but they had started the contest with large losses, whereas Roxie was in the black from the beginning. Her total dollar profit was therefore ahead of theirs. And yet her father sat here bragging his lips loose over what his *boys* had done. She felt a warm sensation creeping up her neck, spreading a flush over her cheeks as it did so. Daddy, you're impossible, she thought. What is it going to take before you notice the job *I'm* doing for you?

"What's that?" George said, lumbering to his feet. "I didn't hear what you said."

"I said Hamlin is really coming along," Roxie said, shuffling the papers on her desk.

"You're sure looking pretty today," George said as he stepped to the door. "What kind of material do you call that?" he asked, admiring her striped dress.

"Spun silk. Very expensive."

"Worth every dime," George said, shrugging off the cost. "The boys will feast their eyes on you at the meeting this afternoon. Should get them working even harder."

All at once Roxie lost interest in the scheduled executive meeting, with its inevitable swaggering and puffing and self-congratulation. She was tired of smiling and winking and sparkling, damn it! But those monthly meetings were sacred, and George never allowed any of the corporate officers to be absent.

He paused in the doorway, a happy smile on his

face. "Yes, ma'am, you sure do your old daddy proud when you look so pretty, Roxie."

Her eyes fell to the financial statement on her desk. Her profits stood at an 80 percent increase, yet Daddy was only proud of her looks. She felt a dull ache in the general vicinity of her heart. "Daddy, what if I skip the meeting this afternoon?" she asked in a tentative voice. "I know you want everybody there, but—"

"Why, that's fine, baby. I know you get tired of those boring old meetings. Why don't you run down to Neiman's and buy yourself a new dress? Just get back in time to come in and model it for us. Boys wouldn't want to miss seeing you today." He reached in his pocket and peeled off several large bills. "If this isn't enough, charge it to me," he said, handing her the money and heading out the door without a backward glance.

She picked up the money and dropped it in her purse. Just wait till you get the bill for today's shopping trip, Daddy, she thought angrily, swallowing past a lump in her throat.

She glanced again at the monthly report. So you're really proud of your "boys," are you, Daddy? Maybe it's time your baby girl made you sit up and take notice. She picked up her telephone and placed a call to Chicago.

The month passed in a blur of activity, and Roxie never left the office at night before ten o'clock. Sometime early in the month she found time to call Todd Kendrick and struck a bargain with him to have half his department's profits credited to her division in exchange for persuading her friend Nita Fancher to let

Todd develop the Fancher ranch. Though Todd grumbled that it was highway robbery, in the end he decided that half of something was better than all of nothing. Since he couldn't make the deal on his own, he had little choice but to share the profits with Roxie. Their relationship became an armed truce. Other than that one short conference, Roxie avoided Todd completely and immersed herself in company business.

As the month wore on, she knew that she'd been right to make the call to Chicago. An old friend from the bank there had steered her onto a lucrative project, and within days she'd committed Sunshine Enterprises to a joint venture with several other big investors developing low-cost housing throughout the Sun Belt.

It was a huge financial undertaking that her father's company could never handle on its own and involved a total projected expenditure of two hundred million dollars. By committing a share of two million dollars, Sunshine Enterprises would receive one percent of the profits of the joint venture. Roxie estimated that the rate of return would be over 25 percent due to the increased leverage held by the joint venture. And best of all, low-cost housing was much faster to develop and sell than the exclusive wealth-focused projects which Sunshine Enterprises normally invested in. Profits started rolling in almost immediately. By month's end, Roxie's division led all others in the company, with Todd now in second place with initial profits from the Fancher ranch; Rusty and Julian had slipped to third place, with the other divisions trailing far behind.

There were a lot of glum faces around the conference table at the July executive meeting. The contest was half over, and the VP's were exhausted from three months of the grueling, nonstop effort to win. Standings had gone up and down like Yo-Yos, and uncertainty and frustration added to fatigue made everybody irritable. Only Roxie was her usual cheerful, vivacious self, but this month the men took no pleasure in her charms. It was too much to be flirted with by someone who had trounced your socks off.

It was a very short meeting, and most of the men kept their heads down while George tried in vain to exhort them onward and upward; he finally realized that he was wasting his breath. "OK, guys, let's call it quits for today," he said with an exasperated sigh, and they were on their feet and out the door before he could change his mind.

Roxie headed straight for her office to get a tissue to wipe away the angry tears that were forming behind her eyes. Not one word of congratulations had George given her for her dazzling performance. No, all he could do was try to shore up the faltering egos of his male executives and give her a half-hearted compliment on the striking black-and-white linen outfit she was wearing. Why didn't he comment that her profits were the highest in the company's history? There was no way she could hope to top this month's profits, and even her most strenuous efforts hadn't earned his praise.

Daddy, Daddy, she whimpered in her empty office. Why isn't there any way to please you? Am I nothing but a little doll to you, someone to dress up and spoil but never consider a real live person? If I'm nothing but a plaything to you, how am I ever going to be real to myself? I don't even know who I am any more.

A rap at the door interrupted her confused thoughts. Before she could call out a response, the door opened, and Todd Kendrick said, "Can I come in for a minute?"

"I was just leaving," Roxie answered, rising from her chair, wanting to avoid both the excitement and the anger that he always aroused in her.

"I won't keep you long," he said, moving toward a chair beside her desk. "I just wanted to congratulate you for the nice job your division did last month. I was impressed with the profits you rolled up."

"Oh," Roxie said, surprise making her breath expel with a soft sound. "I didn't suppose anybody noticed."

Todd laughed. "They noticed, all right. Didn't you see all those long faces? Julian's chin was almost in his lap."

"Oh, Julian, pooh."

Todd gave her a careful look. Didn't she care about Julian's opinion of her work? She'd seemed genuinely pleased at his own compliment. "Your joint venture was a brilliant idea," Todd said, steering the conversation onto her work so he could gauge her reactions. "The company's never tried anything like that before."

"Why, thank you," she answered. She felt a warm glow to have finally earned the praise of someone she respected, and recognition from Todd helped to take away the negative feelings left by her father. A rosy blush crept up her delicate cheekbones, and she paused, hesitant whether to hurry Todd from the office as she'd originally intended.

He watched the play of color across her cheeks, the shy confusion as her eyes evaded his. What had happened to her self-assurance? She usually projected the image of a regal princess far above commoners like himself, yet now he sensed something wistful in her, not aristocratic at all but troubled and vulnerable.

"I thought it was worth going after," Roxie answered, deciding there was no need to terminate an interesting conversation. She sat down and motioned Todd into a chair. "Financing a joint venture with that many parties is pretty complicated, but there's so much leverage that the returns are really impressive."

"You can say that again," Todd said, slumping back in his chair and loosening his tie. "I don't see how the other divisions can hope to catch up with yours. Good thing you're not in the contest!"

"Why, how kind of you to say so, Todd. I have to admit that something inside me loves competition, and I can't help wanting to win." She smiled enchantingly, and Todd could see why men fell all over themselves to claim her attention. He felt a warmth rush through him and remembered the feel of her in his arms, her body soft and fragrant.

"Look, why don't we grab a bite to eat," he said, suddenly wanting more time to get to know her. She was delightful when she was being herself instead of bopping someone in the head with her queen's scepter. The twinkle in Roxie's deep blue eyes found its way to his heart, and a warm smile formed on his lips.

Roxie caught her breath. She'd never seen Todd with a real smile before. At his best he'd looked unhappy, at his worst he'd worn a scowl. "Why, Todd Kendrick," she exclaimed. "I didn't know you were so handsome. Try that again, why don't you?"

His next smile melted some of the ice that had been frozen inside Todd since his wife left him, and it felt so good to him, so pleasantly warm, that it got wider and wider. His smile broke the tension, and they fell into a laughing fit, like schoolkids at play. One of them would manage to stop, but the other would giggle again, and they laughed and laughed until tears streamed down their cheeks. Todd held his sides and rolled his body back and forth, and in sputtering gasps asked, "Will you please tell me what's so funny?"

Roxie wiped her cheeks and fell back in her chair, exhausted and out of breath. "Your smile," she said, wheezing with the effort to talk. "It's always been a lopsided twist of your lips like one of those mad killers in a horror movie. Any time you smiled I knew I'd better run for cover because you planned to sharpen your ax on my neck."

"Such a pretty neck, too," Todd said, the warmth from Roxie's smile spreading through his body like wildfire. Not since the day his ex-wife Jocelyn had left had he felt any affection toward a woman, but the laughter he'd shared with Roxie had been therapeutic. It had carried away his buried anger and bitterness, and he felt cleansed and whole, himself again for the first time in ten months.

He was surprised to find himself free of his incessant heartache and grateful to Roxie for making him feel young again. All at once he wanted to sweep her into his arms and squeeze her in a big, affectionate bear hug. He got up and started toward her.

Roxie saw him coming and couldn't mistake the gleam in his eye. She knew she ought to pull together her lapsed defenses, but how could she bristle and push away the man who'd made her laugh with the carefree abandon of a child? Instead she rose and stretched out her arms, welcoming his embrace.

He held her so tightly she could scarcely breathe, his face buried in her neck, and rocked her back and forth while her toes dangled above the floor.

"You're crazy, do you know that?" she asked, her laughter muffled against his shoulder.

"So I've been told," he said, not at all chagrined. "Now what about that bite to eat?"

"I don't eat sandwiches," she answered. "Too fattening."

"Why didn't you tell me?" he asked, remembering the night he'd taken her to the barbecue stand.

"Why didn't you notice?" She turned her face so that her thick, curly lashes brushed against his cheek. Up close she was so beautiful she took his breath away, and he brushed his lips against her tawny hair.

"Guess I better put you down," he said, rumpling her hair as he did so. "I lose my train of thought when you're so near."

"Sometimes I have a different effect on you. Make you run straight for the door."

He tilted her chin and brushed his nose against hers. "That's on the days when you wear that skunk perfume of yours."

They laughed, totally at ease together for the first time. Roxie thought how nice it was to be close, familiar, without sexuality. Usually her relationships with men involved a high degree of flirtation with sexual overtones, flirtation that brought approving responses and promised more than it delivered—but also built walls that kept her safe inside. She'd been afraid to step outside those walls and let anyone know her as she really was. And yet with Todd, at this moment, she'd let down her barriers and found she liked being herself with him. He respected her work and approved of her as a person, not just as an object of beauty. Best of all, it was a relief not to flirt and cajole.

She sighed happily. "Follow me home and I'll make you a nice, crisp salad with strawberries for dessert."

By the time Todd reached Roxie's door and rang the bell, she'd already changed into a pair of blue sweats. "Come on in," she said, taking the quart of ice cream he'd stopped to buy on the way there. "I hope you don't mind having a drink while I do my exercises. I need to do them before I eat."

Her tiny frame was lost in the oversized sweats, and Todd was taken aback at the change in her. She was more like a rough-and-tumble child than a hard-bitten career woman. "Go right ahead," he said, grinning. "I make a mean Bloody Mary."

He followed her to the refrigerator while she put away the ice cream and removed some celery sticks from the crisper. "Here," she said, "you can use these for swizzle sticks."

He went to the wet bar and began mixing their drinks, but Roxie called, "Make mine a Virgin Mary. I don't want the extra calories."

She flipped on her video tape recorder and positioned herself on the white carpet in front of the television set. As soon as the program began, she bent, kicked, stretched and rolled until she grunted with exertion. When the program ended twenty minutes later, she lay on the floor for a moment, winded, trying to catch her breath.

"That was quite a workout," Todd said, noting her litheness. "You're pretty good."

"I have to keep with it, though, or I get so stiff I can't move." She lifted herself to a sitting position and leaned back against the sofa. "That's why I do it as soon as I come home from work. I set the timer on my VCR and it records the program at noon every day so it's ready and waiting for me."

"A daily regimen like that takes a lot of discipline." He sipped his drink, realizing that she was a more complicated personality than just a spoiled little rich girl, as he'd originally thought.

She fluffed her hair away from her sweat-streaked face. "Has to be done, though. I was cursed with small bones and a short frame, so there's no place to hide fat. Never in my whole life have I been able to gorge myself on a banana split or skip my exercises the way other people do."

Todd mentally reviewed the body now concealed from him in its loose covering and recalled her firm muscles covered by smooth, supple skin. She wasn't bony, as one might expect from such rigid dieting and exercise, but pliant and soft underneath his hands. His fingers trembled on the stem of his glass with the memory. He cleared his throat to ease the tightness behind his Adam's apple. "You've done a good job of taking care of that body of yours," he said roughly.

Roxie swung to her feet in one fluid movement. "I wasn't fishing for compliments," she said, brushing away his words. "I'm not vain about my looks, you know. I just try to keep myself looking good because . . . well, because Daddy expects me to. It makes him proud of me, I guess." She joined Todd at the bar and took a sip of her drink. "Umm, you're right," she said. "You do make a mean Bloody Mary." She took a longer sip. "It really hits the spot on a hot July day."

"And after a good workout."

"How would you know? I'm the one who had the workout."

"Oh, it revved up my engine to watch you," he said in a caressing voice. His arm slipped around her shoulders and pulled her body against his while his lips brushed her temple.

She leaned against him for a moment, then placed her hand on his forearm. "Todd," she said, her words faltering, "I've enjoyed being with you this evening without having to get into any of those male-female games people always play. Couldn't we just be . . . I don't know, *casual* and not get into anything heavy? I'd really like to get to know you better."

"That's just what I had in mind," he said, his fingers gripping her upper arm.

"You know what I mean," Roxie said firmly. "You can always find a lover, but it's hard to find a friend."

Todd didn't like the direction this conversation was going. "Isn't it possible to be both?"

"Not in my limited experience," she insisted.

His lips traveled down the smooth nape of her neck, raising goosebumps of delight. "Let's try it, then. Maybe we can be the first." He reached out and lightly tapped her forehead. "Knock, knock," he said, his voice a gentle whisper. "Is anybody home? I'd like to meet the woman who lives here."

Her fingers found the front of his shirt and clung. "I'm afraid there's nobody there."

"Oh, you're wrong about that," he answered reassuringly.

"How do you know?" she asked, with a tremor in her voice.

"I'm sure I saw a light that meant someone is home."

She tried to laugh, but it came out more like a hiccough.

"I'd be happy to check for occupancy," he said, stroking her cheek with his thumb. A playful smile lit all the dark shadows in his face and made Roxie's heart go flip-flop. She burrowed her head against his chest, luxuriating in the strength of his arms around her. What would it be like, to know someone as a friend . . . but with a greater intimacy? Did she dare let Todd know her that well? "Roxie," he whispered, tilting her face toward his with fingers that were warm and strong. Desire glittered in his dark eyes, their gold flecks now beckoning her to follow him to a new relationship, precarious perhaps but also heart-stirring and rapturous beyond measure.

Roxie brushed her lips against the fingers at her cheek. "Oh, Todd," she murmured, her smile glorious as she parted her lips for his kiss. "You're a most welcome guest."

Her skin tasted of salt and sweat, inciting Todd's desire, and his tongue probed against the barrier of her teeth until she responded, letting him plunge hungrily into her mouth. Their kiss was a splendor of sensation, and they clung to one another, not breathing, only greedily devouring until their hearts pounded with shared passion.

Roxie felt the rock-hard bones of Todd's ribcage as he crushed her against him, the pressure of his hands against her back. The room was full of the spicy fragrance of candles burning on a coffee table nearby, yet Roxie's nostrils were more conscious of the musky male scent of Todd's skin than of the perfumed air. After what seemed an eternity they pulled apart, chests heaving, to suck in air, then immediately fell into another deep kiss that made them light-headed and dizzy.

"Oh, baby, baby," Todd whispered, his fingers slipping underneath her sweatshirt to explore the soft curves of her breast.

"Don't call me that," she protested, even as her body tingled at his touch. "That's what Daddy calls me."

Todd laughed softly. "Believe me, my feelings for you are anything but paternal." His hands found the hem of her sweatshirt and in one swift motion pulled it upward to expose the creamy skin of her breast. His head bent as his hands cupped underneath the warm, rounded flesh and lifted its peak to his mouth. He kissed her nipple to a rosy, dimpled firmness, and as she sighed and ran her fingers through his thick hair, he moved his face across her body, searching for her other breast.

"Todd," she whispered, her body twisting as a soft ache spread through the center of her being.

In one movement he lowered her to the carpeted

floor and yanked the sweatshirt over her head. She lay crosswise underneath him, the carpet soft and plush against her bare skin, and ran her fingers across his shoulders.

He spoke her name, and it was poetry on his lips. Her blue eyes, dark as midnight, dilated with desire when he lowered his head to let his mouth bring tormenting pleasure to her breasts, kissing and nipping, then sucking deeply until she was quivering, sweetly aching all over. She moaned in his arms, and he raised his head to lick a drop of sweat from her upper lip.

"Todd," she whispered again, stretching her torso against him. Shyly she hesitated, then reached out a slender arm to bring his head back to her breast, desperately eager for more of the rapturous sensations he lavished upon her.

His tongue found her nipple and toyed with it, teasing and darting, stretching it slightly with his teeth.

"More," she whispered.

He laughed. "So you like that, do you?" His fingers kneaded her soft skin, lightly pinched her willing nipple, then lifted it to his mouth again. "Well, that makes two of us." His lips closed with a warm, wet suction that made her tremble with ecstasy.

She felt a roaring in her ears that drowned out the sounds of the city outside. She whispered words she'd never said before into Todd's ear, then heard them whispered back in an urgent, demanding rhythm. Her body became a shimmering torch under his mouth and hands, and she thrust upward to meet his touch until she thought she would explode from frenzied excitement. She luxuriated in the pleasure of his mouth, her nipples swollen and tingling, until the sweet ache spread downward with a melting sensation. "Todd, Todd," she murmured, her fingers clutching at his back.

His fingers crept inside the waistband of her sweatpants, then down, and he kissed her eyelids, chuckling softly.

"What's so funny?" she asked, trembling as his mouth found its way to her earlobe and his tongue licked, his teeth nipped.

His fingers made their way to her secret place with sensuous strokes that made her quiver. "You are," he said, his fingers probing higher until she gasped.

"Todd, no," she protested. "Nobody ever—"

He caught her hands as they moved to shield herself from him. "Put your hands back where they were," he said, placing them around his waist. "I like for you to hold me tight."

His knowing mouth moved back to her breast, sure now of her melting response, and gently sucked until she relaxed in his arms, moaning softly. He began to speak in broken phrases, breathing heavily as he told her how beautiful she was, how she excited him, until she was caught up in a cloud of passion, mesmerized by the sound of his voice.

"Hold me, Roxie," he commanded, and while she clung to him, his finger made a second intimate journey. Too lost in wonder to resist, she let him perform his magic until, eyes closed, she began to move against him, caught in a vortex of desire that spiraled higher and higher. "That's it, let go," he said, his breath raspy against her ear. His head dropped and he found her nipple, sucking until it became a plump, ripe raspberry in his mouth. A soft cry sounded in her throat and her fingers tangled in his hair. His mouth moved back to hers, his tongue sweetly plundering, and with one last, masterful stroke of his fingers, her back arched and she cried aloud as a spasm of total joy swept through her, melting every barrier and carrying her to the height of human release. When it ended, she collapsed against him, her face luminous with sweat and pleasure, her eyes darkly mysterious.

"Todd, what was—" she started to ask, then broke off in confusion.

"Don't you know?" he teased.

She put her hands over her reddened cheeks. "But you didn't—"

"That was for you. We still have plenty of time," he said, lowering her hands to touch him. He kissed her lightly on the lips, then sat up and began to unbutton his shirt.

"I'm embarrassed," she said, crossing her arms over her breasts. "You still have on all your clothes."

"Yes, and some of them are a little tighter now than they were when I came in here tonight," he said, grinning as he shrugged off his shirt. "Come here and see what you can do about that, will you?" He scooped her body over his and nuzzled her neck. "God, Roxie, you're so beautiful," he said in wonder as he gazed reverently at the spill of her bare breasts above him. He pulled her against him, delighting in the feel of her flesh against his own. Her fingers began to work in the mat of hair on his chest, tugging gently, as she brushed his eyelids and cheeks with feathery kisses.

Just as he was about to pull her into a deep, passionate kiss, the telephone shrilled.

"Let it ring," he said, reaching for her.

"Ummm," she answered, parting her lips and flicking her tongue against his. Her fingers found the buckle of his pants and loosened it, then moved downward. "Ummm," she sighed again as his tongue grazed the roof of her mouth.

But the telephone continued to shrill.

"It must be something important," she said, sadly breaking their embrace. "I'd better answer it."

"No," he growled. "The telephone can wait. I can't." He pulled her hand to the front of his trousers and thrust against it, then caught her hair and pulled her backward into a deep, ravenous kiss that sent her senses reeling.

Still the telephone shrilled. "Todd, it must have rung fifteen times," Roxie said.

He sat up in disgust. "Go ahead and answer it. But hurry back."

She hurried across the room to the telephone, her hips swaying gracefully in the sweatpants, her full breasts exposed to Todd's devouring glance. He was flooded with desire at her unconsciously sensual movements. Then in dismay he watched the transformation in her as the person on the other end of the line began to discuss a business deal.

It was a long telephone call, and by the time she hung up the receiver fifteen minutes later, her mind was far away. It was almost in surprise that she realized Todd was still there, and when she looked down and saw her nude torso, she scrambled to retrieve her sweatshirt and pull it over her head.

"What's going on with you?" he asked, standing to take her in his arms again.

"That was Phoenix, calling about the joint venture," she said. "We've got a chance to buy a big tract, but everybody is going to have to come up with some more money right away."

"Can't it wait until tomorrow?" He pulled her into his arms and began to run his hands down her body.

"Now, Todd, you know how joint ventures are. It's a type of partnership where everybody is liable for the debts of the venture. We have to come up with our share immediately. I'll have to call my banker friend at home in Chicago and get a bigger credit line set up to take care of the new investment."

"You don't have to call him right this minute," he argued. He lowered his mouth to hers, but her response was absentminded, and he realized that even if her body was in his arms, her mind was far away. Determined to bring her attention back to him, he tried to kiss her, but Roxie didn't respond.

"Todd," she murmured, having thought up a solution while he was distracted with her body. "Let me make a couple of quick calls and take a shower. Then I'll fix that salad I promised you, and after we've had a nice dinner, we can cuddle up on the couch and do anything you like."

"Business before pleasure, is that it?" he said in a hard voice.

"Something like that. I need to catch my friend in Chicago before it gets any later. That way he can wire the letter of credit for me first thing in the morning."

Todd's hands fell to his side in disgust. "I'll tell you what, Roxie. Why don't you just cuddle up with the telephone, because I don't intend to stick around until you make time for me in between your damned appointments!"

"Todd, please," Roxie said, as though she were trying to reason with a recalcitrant child. "It won't take long, and I have to do this so my division can stay ahead."

"So your division can stay ahead of what?" Todd's voice was rising steadily.

"Why, in the contest, of course."

"Damn it, Roxie, your division isn't even in the contest," he barked. "Don't you remember, sweetheart, you're not a contestant, you're the prize."

"Is that so?" she answered, jerking away from him. "Well, let me tell you something. My division is going to be in the number one position when this contest is over, and if you don't like it, you can damn sure drop out of the race, because I don't intend to change just for the sake of your precious male ego." Her eyes were blazing sparks that should have melted anything within ten feet but only spurred Todd to greater anger.

"Ambitious, ha! Ambush is what you ought to call it, double-crossing your own colleagues and lining up deals behind their backs. If there's anything I can't stand, it's an aggressive female who thinks she's got to prove herself to the whole world!"

"Oh, you fine, upstanding model citizen, you. Why,

all you are is a caveman who wants to club a woman into submission!"

Club her into submission? Is that what she thought of his tender lovemaking half an hour ago, when he'd held back his own pleasure to—"Let me tell you something, Roxie," he said, his words searing her heart like molten lava. "A caveman wanted sex from his woman. All I want from you is your father's money!" Todd stuffed his shirttail back into his pants and stalked out the door, slamming it behind him.

Roxie collapsed on the sofa, her face contorted with tears. Eventually she remembered the telephone call that had precipitated their argument, and forcing a bright smile onto her face, she walked across the room and dialed her friend in Chicago.

Chapter Six

Todd spent a miserable evening with an ache in his groin and fury in his heart. Damn Roxie, anyway. She was nothing but one big tease, flirting with a man till she had him so hot and bothered he couldn't see straight, then—

He slammed through kitchen cabinets and drawers, throwing together something to eat that would satisfy his physical appetite even though he was still tormented with sexual hunger. He took a huge T-bone steak from the freezer and stuck the cold slab under the broiler, then opened up a can of pork and beans and ate from the can while he was waiting for the meat to cook. He wasn't even surprised when the steak caught fire in the broiler and filled his kitchen with thick clouds of smoke. That's just about my luck tonight, he thought, and gave himself up to bitter thoughts while he ate the most unappetizing meal he'd ever seen in his life. He left the kitchen in an absolute mess and poured himself a stiff drink, trying to anesthetize his emotions with loud music on the stereo. When that didn't work he tried a nerve-deadening late movie on television, but at 1:00 A.M. he was still wide awake, muscles twitching and mind racing. He tried reading a popular suspense novel, but the book was such a bore he finally threw it at the wall in disgust. It hit with a satisfying thud, however, so he grabbed another book and threw that, too. He finally had to quit when his neighbor in the apartment upstairs pounded on the floor with a broom. With that, Todd yanked off his clothes and threw himself across the bed, hoping he'd eventually be able to sleep.

His argument with Roxie had stirred up old feelings, and he lay on the bed remembering times when he'd made love to Jocelyn, his ex-wife. She'd been superficial and vain, he knew that when he married her, but there'd been a sexual chemistry between them that had kept their marriage alive for a long time. She'd never shared an interest in his work, only in his paycheck, and no matter how much he made, it was never enough for her growing demands. Yet she'd been such a clever manipulator that she'd used sex as a lure, urging him on, her favors increasing as his salary grew. No wonder he set new records at Sunshine Enterprises, Todd thought bitterly; George Lyons would never know how great a debt he owed Jocelyn Kendrick for the motivation she'd given Todd. She'd kept Todd eating out of her hand for ten years, until he'd gone about as far at Sunshine as she could reasonably expect, and then she looked around for someone with more money. It hadn't taken her long, either.

The old feeling of rejection washed over Todd with the same force as on the day she'd left him. His ego had taken a battering that he'd once thought could never be overcome. He'd loved Jocelyn and supposed she loved him. Or if he didn't love her, he desired her, and physical passion was a good enough substitute for love. It had never occurred to him that she would be unfaithful, and he experienced afresh the metallic iron taste that had risen in his mouth when she'd flaunted her affair with the Oklahoma oil baron who was her new lover. Todd cringed now to think how he'd entreated her to stay with him. He'd lost all his pride, humbled himself, and she'd scorned him anyway. Months later, when he'd begun to recover, he wondered whether he'd been hurt more by her leaving or by the memory of his own mortification at her hands, with his failure there for all the world to see. He'd vowed that never again would a woman have him at her feet, cracking a whip over his head. No, he'd sworn to be the one holding all the trump cards in the unlikely event that he ever let another woman into his life.

And now look at you, Kendrick, he berated himself. You ended up getting involved with another woman as shallow and selfish as Jocelyn. But even Jocelyn never got away with what Roxie Lyons did to you tonight. *You fool*, you did everything in your power to give Roxie pleasure—and by God, it sure looked like she'd never felt anything like it before, either. She moaned and melted and begged for more

—and then she double-crossed you just like she does everybody else, taking all she could get and giving nothing in return. It would be a cold day in hell before he got any satisfaction from Roxie Lyons. Todd crawled out of bed and went to take a cold shower.

Roxie herself had an equally unpleasant evening. Her telephone call to Chicago made short shrift of the dazzling smile she'd plastered on, and all her coaxing and wheedling fell on deaf ears. Her banker was adamant: He couldn't approve additional credit until his own supervisor reviewed a new corporate financial statement. Sunshine Enterprises had been in the news too often lately with big purchases and sales, and the bank didn't know how much credit the company's current financial strength would support. "Hell, Roxie," Tim said, "your company has been so fluid the past three months, I bet your own treasurer doesn't know what you're worth."

"Oh, yes, he does, right down to the penny," she insisted, and rattled off a figure that was within fifty cents of the current net value.

"Well, in that case, it won't be any problem to set up a credit line twice what you're asking for. Just send me the financial statement, and I'll let Harry King sign off on it."

"I'll get it to you by Telex first thing in the morning," she promised.

"No hurry," said Tim, "Harry's in Minnesota on vacation and won't be back till next week."

"Next week? Tim, listen to me, I have to get that money to Phoenix within two days. It's for that joint

venture project. Can't you call him in Minnesota?"
Roxie's pulse raced from her rising anxiety, and her
voice sounded high and thin. Desperate, even.

"He's in a wilderness cabin with no telephone. Said
he wanted a rest where nobody could bother him."

"Then what am I going to do?" she wailed.

"No problem, Roxie. Just temporarily transfer
some funds from your corporate accounts to cover
your draft, and as soon as Harry gets back and signs
off on the loan, you can replace it."

She felt a small glimmer of hope. "I don't
know . . ."

"Nothing to it," Tim insisted. "Just find an account
with a surplus for accrued depreciation or something,
sign a promissory note to the account, get another
corporate officer to approve it, and you'll be covered.
OK?"

"OK," she said, still dubious, but knowing that he
gave her no other choice. She had to have the money,
and soon. "Thanks, Tim. You'll be hearing from me."

She replaced the telephone receiver, her mind
troubled. Maybe she'd pushed her luck too far and it
had been bound to catch up with her. That was one of
the hazards of high-risk deals; sometimes they were
like a house of cards, easily toppled. Yet the Phoenix
joint venture was sound, and there was no reason to
pull out just because of a temporary blip in financing.
If Sunshine withdrew, the company would lose the big
earnings that still lay ahead. They could cut back on
their partnership percentage, but to do so would
mean cutting back on their future revenues. No, she
would have to find a way. She wanted those profits for

her division. She'd show those glory-hounds yet . . . and Daddy, too.

As usual when she was nervous, she paced the floor, and as she wandered around the room she found Todd's tie hanging from a barstool where he'd tossed it when he first arrived, while he was mixing their drinks. Todd! She'd forgotten all about him in her preoccupation with her banking problem. What must he be thinking of her?

Then in a flash it all came back to her . . . his tender, practiced lovemaking, like nothing she'd ever experienced in her life. She'd had an affair from time to time, when there was someone special she'd wanted to please, but it had never been like this before. Other men had been so aroused by her beauty that they'd had little control of their performance and no consideration for her. Roxie had never figured out what all the fuss was about where sex was concerned, because it seemed to consist of a few fumblings and gropings and then a heavy body collapsed across hers. She'd learned that moist kisses and a few deft movements of her hand would hasten the process considerably and leave the gentleman in question her grateful and devoted ally. Sex had been nothing but another useful gadget in her arsenal of tools. She'd had no idea that . . .

She remembered the exciting feel of Todd's mouth and hands. Until tonight she'd never thought of her body as anything but a frame for modeling clothes—until Todd had brought it to life and made it sing with joy.

She dropped onto the floor, a soft smile on her face,

and stretched her arms in sheer pleasure. Todd, you're so wonderful! she thought, her happiness radiating in the room. She got up to go to the telephone and call him, and she dialed the first three digits of Todd's number before she remembered the bitter fight they'd had and his storming out the door. Her total preoccupation with the urgent business matter had blocked the entire scene from her mind.

What had he yelled at her? Something that infuriated her at the time, but what was it? She worked her mind through the entire argument, and with a shudder heard his words shouted back at her from memory: "A caveman wanted sex from his woman. All I want from you is your father's money!" Todd, no, she whimpered in the empty room. It isn't true, you don't mean that. But he did, he did. He'd told her he intended to win the contest. She'd mistakenly thought he wanted to prove himself to her. How naive she'd been. He didn't give a fig for her opinion of him. He didn't want her, he wanted her father's *money*.

She shuddered involuntarily, like someone waking from a bad dream to find that the dream was real. Her body still trembled with the memory of his lovemaking, and her first thought was that she'd placated lots of angry men in her day. It wouldn't be hard to win him back . . . if she wanted him back. And something inside her ached to know again the sweetness of his touch. In a way she could understand why he was furious with her; she'd left him unsatisfied because of her single-minded obsession with business. She could make it up to him—if she wanted to. Though it was new to experience her own sexuality, she knew how to make love to a man. She could give him the same pleasure he'd given her. Yes, she could call him, and he'd come back, and she could spend the whole night making amends for deserting him at such an inappropriate time.

She remembered his throbbing manhood and thought it was no wonder he'd yelled at her. Maybe he had a right to scold her. There was a time and place for being ambitious, and the midst of lovemaking certainly wasn't it.

Roxie dropped her face into her hands and sobbed. She couldn't keep making excuses for him, pretending that what he'd done was all right. Nothing could ever justify those horrible words he'd hurled at her—or take away her sense of shame and betrayal. She'd been stupid to succumb to his embraces and make herself vulnerable to him.

She lifted her head with an angry toss. I won't have it, Todd Kendrick, do you hear me? she shouted silently across the sleeping city. I've never danced to anyone's tune but my own, and I don't intend to start now. I'll find a way, and you'll be dancing a jig to my bagpipe before we're done, do you understand that? Roxie yanked off her sweatclothes and took a shower, then marched herself into the kitchen and ate a whole bowlful of ice cream.

Roxie spent the next morning in the treasurer's office pouring over the corporate books, searching for an account with surplus funds which she could borrow temporarily. There were several possibilities, but most of them would require permission from the treasurer himself, a dour, arch-conservative type who was affronted by anything he considered a raid on the corporate treasury. She could probably go over his head to Daddy, but Daddy was unpredictable and might resent her jumping channels. Her eye kept coming back time after time to a separate account held by Todd's division, with a substantial fund set aside for development of the Florida beachfront. The money was in an interest-bearing account waiting for the day when a hotel chain should buy part of the property, with Sunshine to develop a resort area around the hotel site. It might be weeks or even months before the money was needed.

Roxie leaned back in the treasurer's leather chair and tapped a pencil against her chin. If she handled it just right, she could persuade Todd to let her borrow from his account. He was mad last night when he left her, but considering the frustrated state he was in, he would probably be quite susceptible to her ploys. After the ugly things he'd said to her, she welcomed the opportunity to get revenge. Maybe she could even tie up his money indefinitely and sabotage any possibility that he might win the contest. He mustn't win! She couldn't bear to be married to a man whose only interest was her father's bank account. She quickly left the treasurer's office and went back to her own to freshen her makeup and spray a little perfume behind her ears. All right, Todd Kendrick, here I come, ready or not, she thought, giving Lorraine a merry wave of her hand as she left the office.

Even though Todd was wary of her, Roxie was so charmingly apologetic that he wanted to believe her breathless explanation for her behavior the night before. She wore a deceptively simple dress of soft blue cotton that contoured her bosom and swirled around her hips as she swayed on tiptoe, hands clasped in front of her, beside his desk. He caught the scent of her perfume and remembered the way it had clung to her body as she lay underneath him, delighting his nostrils as his lips had . . . He swore softly when he felt a familiar warmth spread outward from his groin.

"Please, Todd, say you'll let me make amends for, well, for my inexcusable behavior." Her smile would have melted an arctic glacier, and a delicious shrug of her shoulders rippled her breasts, outlining their firm tips. He clenched his fists to prevent himself from reaching out to touch her. He knew it was rude, but he'd purposely remained sitting when she breezed into his office. Good thing he wasn't standing right now, the way his body was reacting to hers. It would be pretty damned embarrassing. Todd cleared his throat and motioned her into a chair. She sat down and leaned across on one elbow so that her breasts spilled forward and he could see her cleavage at the deep V-neck. "Well?" she asked, her eyes twinkling at him. "Do you?"

He cleared his throat again. Her dress was the exact deep sky-blue of her eyes. "Do I what?" he asked hoarsely.

Just like taking candy from a baby, Roxie thought serenely, shifting slightly in the chair while she watched his eyes follow the supple motion of her breasts. "Do you forgive me and say you'll let me . . . make it up to you?" Her smoky eyes conveyed a sensual message, promising untold delights. Her tongue darted out and flicked a naughty circle around her lips, and she shifted in the chair again, crossing her shapely legs, then running a long fingernail down her calf.

"What do you have in mind?" he asked, eyes narrowed in exquisite agony as desire ripped through him.

"Why don't we just pretend last night never happened and start all over?" she purred.

Todd was like a drowning man, almost sucked under by the currents of her voice, her fragrance, her beauty, but he still had a small shred of rationality left to analyze her words. He barked in amused laughter. "Are you so sure you want to forget *everything* that happened last night?" His gold-flecked eyes were as smoky and mysterious as her own. He remembered all too well the way her body had become a musical instrument, responding melodiously to the mastery of his hands.

She blushed prettily and experienced a warm sensation of her own. Taking Todd's money was one task that would have some exciting fringe benefits. Maybe after she had him moaning with pleasure and his signature on the dotted line, he would . . . She blushed again and felt her nipples harden in anticipation. "Maybe we'll find our next time together will be . . . mutually satisfying," she said huskily, squirming in her seat to ease the not unpleasant ache she felt there.

The silence lengthened and Roxie waited while he scrutinized her, trying to bore through to her soul. He didn't want to let her make a fool out of him again, but God, how he wanted her. Could he trust her? Probably not. His eyes drank in her smooth, glowing skin, her tantalizing curves. It was his turn to squirm in his seat. He'd been burned too many times by Jocelyn not to recognize that Roxie was using the same tactics on him. But Roxie wasn't Jocelyn, and even if she had some of the same traits, she might not . . . Todd ran his fingers across his chin and narrowed his eyes. Maybe he shouldn't judge her too quickly. "When?" he said gruffly.

A sensuous smile played across Roxie's berry-colored lips. She mustn't seem to be in a hurry. He'd taken the bait, but she hadn't landed him yet. "Your choice," she said. "What about sometime next week?" She lifted a slim arm to brush her shoulder-length hair away from her face, knowing that the stretch of her body accentuated her breasts.

Was she toying with him? Why next week? If she really meant to make good the promises she was signaling, why wait? She'd had a taste of the pleasure he could offer and ought to be eager for more. Intrigued with the possibilities, Todd decided to test her sincerity and see if she was making a bona fide offer. "What about tonight?" he rasped.

"I was hoping you'd say that," she said with a silky laugh. She rose in one fluid motion that sent her full skirt swirling around her hips and legs. "You won't go home hungry tonight, Todd, I promise you," she said, blowing him a kiss on her way out the door.

"Roxie," he said, stopping her. When she turned quizzically, he added, "No television exercises tonight. I'll give you a good workout myself."

As the door closed behind her, Todd breathed in the fragrance she'd left behind and sighed. He hoped he wasn't making a big mistake, but he had to give their relationship another chance. It had the potential to be fantastic if they could develop it properly. A good businessman had to learn when a risk was worth taking, and on the job, his batting average was exceptional. Todd grinned and crossed his fingers.

Roxie left the office early that afternoon to go by the German delicatessen on her way home. She wasn't much of a cook, but she had a good eye for color and texture, and she picked out foods that would look attractive on a plate lined with crisp lettuce. As soon as she got home to Turtle Creek, she arranged thick slices of cold beef tenderloin with dollops of horseradish cream, wedges of boiled egg and avocado, sliced beets and cucumbers, and scoops of potato salad. She used parsley and radishes for garnish, then chopped some marinated mushrooms for extra flavor and drizzled them over the avocados. It was a beautiful salad plate for a hot July evening, and maybe after it cooled off they could eat dinner on the terrace. In the meantime she put the plates in the refrigerator to chill along with an expensive bottle of white wine.

She thought she'd planned her strategy carefully and went over it again while she took a long soak in the tub with perfumed bubbles. First they would have a cool drink on the sofa while she softened Todd up with smiles and surreptitious wanderings of her hands. When he began to respond aggressively, she'd hold him off with dinner on the terrace. Thank goodness the roses were blooming. He wouldn't be able to think straight with their intoxicating fragrance. During dessert she'd turn the conversation to business, then when they came back inside to have another drink and cuddle on the couch, she'd wheedle approval for the transfer of funds. After that—. She splashed cool water on her face and smiled. After that, she'd have Todd Kendrick exactly where she wanted him, and anything that happened afterward would be a little extra bonus for her efforts. She lifted herself from the refreshing water and dried her body to a silky perfection, humming softly to herself.

When Todd rang the doorbell at seven o'clock, he was wearing a casual pair of khaki slacks with a rust-and-tan houndstooth check shirt turned back at the cuffs. He was freshly shaved, his hair gleamed like burnished wheat from a thorough brushing, and a spicy-scented aftershave clung to his skin. When he smiled unsuspectingly at Roxie, his brilliant teeth white and even, she felt a momentary qualm of guilt for the way she'd set him up. He looked fresh-scrubbed and innocent, somehow. Then she remembered his hateful words of the previous evening and steeled herself to go on with her plan. It was nothing more than he deserved. If money was all he cared about, what better way to hurt him than in his pocketbook? She smiled, already tasting sweet revenge.

"Come on in," she said with a warm welcome. "I waited to let you mix the drinks. You have such an . . . experienced touch." Her fingers crept out to stroke his hand, big and solid and sun-bronzed against hers. Before he could respond she turned and led him into the living room, her hips swaying in her bright yellow shorts. "How did you get that nice tan?" she asked. "I'm at the office so much I hardly get any sun except on weekends."

"Most of this I got on my trip to Florida last

month," he said, "but I try to play tennis every evening before dark and swim on Saturday afternoons. I'd rather stay in shape that way than with an exercise routine like yours."

She laughed softly. "I thought you told me you'd enjoy a good workout tonight." She felt him lean toward her and sidestepped to the bar. "What are you mixing tonight?" she asked, her voice flirtatious.

"I thought we might try one part male to one part female," he said, grinning. "That's a chemical combination that's been known to conduct electricity since before Ben Franklin flew his kite."

"Maybe I better light some candles in case we blow out a fuse," she whispered, leaning across the bar to stroke his forearm with her long fingernails.

It wasn't easy to evade Todd's pursuit, but Roxie had had lots of past experience and managed to get him to mix the drinks while she dallied just out of reach. The cozy scene on the sofa went just as she'd planned it, with playful hugs and teasing kisses and the promise of more to come. Though Todd insisted she'd whetted his appetite for more than food, she lured him to the terrace, site for the all-important siege. The scent of the roses was lush as dusk fell, and candlelight played on Roxie's skin. She reached for Todd's hand across the table, her fingers rotating over the knuckle of his thumb. Her yellow tanktop revealed more than it concealed, and she made sure to keep her torso in slow motion, her unbound breasts swaying gently with each movement. "Dessert?" she asked.

"What did you have in mind?" he asked, gripping her fingers in his strong hand.

"How about something cold and sweet, like ice cream?"

"How about something warm and sweet, like raspberries," he answered.

"Raspberries?" she asked, puzzled. She noticed that he was gazing at her breasts with a significant expression and felt her nipples pucker as she realized what he meant. "Oh," she murmured, a blush creeping up her cheeks. A warm, languid sensation poured over her, and she realized that she'd better keep her mind on business or the evening might get out of hand. "Maybe we'll leave dessert until later. Why don't we go inside where it's cool and have another drink?"

"Why don't we go inside where it's private and see if we can warm things up?"

"Now, Todd, I promised you wouldn't go home hungry tonight, didn't I?"

"I didn't come here for beef tenderloin, Roxie, even if it was superb." He pushed back his chair and came to her, lifting her with a firm grip on her elbow and steering her inside. "We have some unsettled business from last night, remember?" Her hip brushed against him and he laughed sardonically. "See what I mean?"

All at once he was so close, so big, so strong and muscular that she was overwhelmed. She must have been crazy to think she could keep her own mind clear while she seduced him to get his approval on the transfer of funds. Her body was on the verge of betraying her and bringing all her plans to naught. *Roxie*, get a grip on yourself, she scolded. Fifteen more minutes and the deed will be done. Then you can throw yourself at him and it won't matter. With shaking fingers she closed the door behind them. "I really need another drink," she murmured. "It was too warm on the terrace and I feel light-headed."

Todd laughed in amusement but good-naturedly went to the bar and mixed another round of drinks. Roxie patted a seat beside her on the sofa and hoped Todd had left the alcohol out of her drink. It was going to take all her concentration to bring off this little coup.

Her finger trailed up his arm while she made what seemed to be idle chitchat about the office, and Todd gave indifferent answers while he pulled her against his chest and buried his face in her fragrant hair. "How's your Florida project coming?" she asked, brushing a kiss against his bare collarbone.

"Looks like it's dead in the water for the time being," he said, shifting her body to face him.

"Too bad," she said, taking his hand, then moving it to her breast. She heard a sharp intake of breath, and then his hand slipped under her tanktop to the bare flesh beneath. Her breast, eager for further exploration, quivered expectantly, and he felt her nipple grow taut and firm as his fingers gently stroked her skin. For long moments the room was quiet except for the sound of their rapid breathing, and then Todd bent his head to the hollow of her neck and began to kiss her, his tongue tracing ovals on her skin.

Surprised at the wave of desire that swept through her, Roxie wanted to touch Todd, to know whether he was responding to her with the same urgency.

"Careful," he said, removing her hand. "You're playing with dynamite, Roxie."

"Didn't you like it?" she asked, embarrassed that he might think she'd been too forward.

"Ummm, I sure did," he said, lifting her tanktop and teasing her nipple. "But if we're going to have . . . that *mutual satisfaction* you were talking about . . ." His mouth brushed hers and she could taste the citrus from his drink. He continued, "Then you better let me do the workout. I won't last ten seconds if you do it." His lips darted back to her breast, teasing her while he blew on her nipple with his warm breath.

"That tickles," she said, scooting up in his arms and trying to get her breasts out of his reach. The effect of his touch was magic, with much more impact on her than on him. He was the one who was supposed to be melting with desire while she was the one who was supposed to have the clear head. She lifted herself on her knees so she could reach his ear, then let her tongue slip inside, nipping and licking until she felt his breath coming faster. While he was off-guard, her hand slipped downward and caressed gently until he moaned. When he tried to remove her hand again, she whispered, "Please, I want to."

"Todd," she whispered, licking his earlobe, then taking a tiny bite with her sharp teeth. "Will you do me a favor?"

"Anything," he said in a thick voice. Thinking he knew what she wanted, he lifted her yellow top and pressed his mouth against her breast, sucking in dizzy rhythm to the strokes of her fingers on his column of flesh. "Oh, God, Roxie," he mumbled, lost in a cloud of sensuality.

"Todd," she whispered urgently, knowing that time

was quickly running out on her. Her hand felt seared with his swollen heat; he couldn't last much longer. "Todd, if you're not going to do anything with the Florida property for a while, would you let my division borrow that money you've set aside?" Her fingers continued their slow, exciting strokes, and she took a sharp nip of the tender flesh at his neck.

There was a roaring in Todd's ears as he tried to fight through the thick mists of desire to hear what she'd said. His body was pulsing rapidly toward the point of no return, and some deep, gentlemanly instinct made him stop, draw back, to be sure he satisfied his lady. He groped toward her breast, hidden from him, and reached to pull her underneath him. He tugged at the clothes which interfered with his single-minded determination to thrust himself inside her. He dimly realized that Roxie's hands were preventing him, that she was repeating his name over and over, but the sound came through a faraway haze that didn't penetrate his consciousness.

"Todd, please," she said, desperate to make him hear her before it was too late. Once he'd satisfied himself, he'd never agree to her request. "I asked you if you'd let me borrow the money in your Florida account for a few days until the bank approves my loan."

Groggily he pulled himself above her and forced his eyes to focus. He shook his head to clear it, then asked her to repeat what she'd said. As she did so, he gazed at her, dumbfounded. When he realized what she was asking, fury broke forth inside him, and roughly he pushed her away from him.

"Damn it to hell, Roxie, is that what this is all about?"

"Todd, no," she whispered, reaching out her hand to stroke him again and bring him back to her.

He shoved her hand aside. "Don't touch me," he snarled.

"Todd, you don't understand," she said, fear draining all the color from her face. What had she done? Why was he so overwrought? Hadn't she given him what he wanted? It was a fair exchange, so why was he being unreasonable? God, he looked like a thundercloud! She'd never seen anybody so angry, not even Daddy.

"What do you mean, I don't understand?" he shouted. "I understand entirely too well. I was married to a woman just like you for ten years and I know all about your kind. Women who trade sexual favors for money are nothing new. You're no better than a—"

"Todd, no, you're wrong," she cut in, wondering what had gone wrong with her perfect scheme.

"Let me tell you all about it," he said, angrily, not caring that he was exposing his vulnerability to her. "When I married Jocelyn, I was making $10,000 a year. For that I got a few French kisses and we made love once a week. But the more I made, the more she put out. Last year I made $75,000. Do you know what $75,000 will buy? Sex. Anytime, anyplace, anyhow. There was no limit to what she would dream up—as long as I was raking it in. This year I'll make over $100,000 with my bonuses, but she found a guy worth $10 million, so she ran off with him. What do you suppose he's getting from her, huh?" Fury made Todd's voice shake, yet the words continued to pour out in a searing flood. "How much is it you need, Roxie? $150,000? God, surely you're not so dumb as to think you can get that much with a few kisses. Come here, baby, show me your whole bag of tricks, because it's going to take all of them to get that money you want so badly. I've been put through the wringer, and I've learned the hard way how to get my money's worth."

He grabbed her in his arms and pulled her into a deep kiss, his tongue and teeth assaulting her mouth, his hands gripping her soft flesh. She began to whimper and tried to pull away, frightened at this cruel side of him, frightened even more by the awful revelation he'd made.

"Don't tell me any more," she cried, putting her hands over her ears. "I don't want to hear it." She began to weep, her face contorted.

Todd stood up and straightened his clothes, then angrily zipped his pants. He'd said too much, but he hadn't said it all. "Welcome to the real world, princess, to the place where real people love and hate and get so hurt they don't know how they're going to keep on living. What do you think I am, anyway? Some sucker you can con because he's nothing but male hormones you can fire up and play with? I'm a person, Roxie. Sure, I wanted you. But damn it, I wanted *you,* not your company, not your ambition, not your money, not even your beautiful body. I wanted to make contact with a person, a real, live, breathing woman."

"Todd, I'm sorry, please," she said, dropping her

head in her lap while the stinging tears continued to fall.

"Yeah. So am I." He walked across the room to the door, then turned and said in a sad, empty voice, "Roxie, you didn't have to go through all this. If you wanted the money, why didn't you just ask me? I'd have given it to you. You didn't have to buy me with your body." He closed the door without a sound and walked away, his footsteps a hollow echo in the summer air.

Chapter Seven

*R*oxie huddled in a heap on the couch, unable to stop the flow of tears. Everything had gone wrong, so wrong, and she didn't know what to do about it. What she'd intended as a clever strategem to get Todd's cooperation had turned into a needle-sharp weapon that had pierced his ego to the quick. He'd shouted at her in an angry voice that did nothing to hide his wounded pride. When he'd realized she'd been using him, he was devastated. "Todd, I didn't mean it the way you think," she whispered brokenly into the emptiness. "I wanted you, too, but I couldn't let myself give in to those feelings until I got you to . . ."

Even to Roxie the words were inadequate. There was no way to explain it away, not even to herself. What she'd done had been unpardonable, and whether she'd intended it or not, someone had gotten hurt. Someone. *Todd* had gotten hurt. She buried her head in her hands and cried some more.

But why had it all gone sour? What she'd done tonight really wasn't so different from the way she always flirted with men, rousing their interest with smiles and flattery until they were eating out of her hand. They got their egos stroked, and in return she enjoyed a sense of power. It was a game where everybody knew the rules, and nobody got hurt. Except Todd. He didn't realize it was a game and took it seriously. But why? After all, he was getting what he wanted. It was a fair exchange, wasn't it?

Besides, Todd wasn't exactly a pillar of virtue himself. After all, he'd shouted at her that all he wanted was her father's money. It was a vicious remark that pierced her to the quick. Roxie shook her head, trying to clear away her confusion, and knew deep down inside that Todd didn't really mean those hateful words. He'd only lashed out in anger. Otherwise she'd never have hurt him the way she did tonight. No, he'd wanted a lot more from her than her father's money, and she'd played him for a fool.

Roxie went into the bathroom and splashed her blotchy face with cold water. Her eyes were swollen, and mascara had dissolved in her tears and left black streaks down her cheeks. Face it, Roxanne Lyons, she said to her miserable reflection. You pulled a cheap, low-down trick, and there's no way in the world you can rationalize it. Oh, you'd like to justify yourself and pretend it was all Todd's fault for taking it too seriously. You'd like to ease your conscience and crawl back under a rock so you won't have to remember the anguished look on his face. God, Roxie, you tore the heart right out of him. The one thing you didn't count on was that the guy is decent, clear to the core. He'd never treat you as an object to be manipulated, and it never occurred to Todd that you'd have any less respect for him.

Roxie was flooded with a sense of shame unlike anything she'd experienced in her entire life. It oozed like hot tar into every cell of her conscience, smearing and staining until she wanted to cry aloud from the ignominy. She went into the bathroom and stood under the shower until all the hot water was gone, yet still felt unclean when she stepped out to dry herself. Wasn't there any way to make amends and relieve this tormenting guilt?

She tossed in the bed, haunted by restless dreams. In one dream she was being pursued by something evil, but though she tried to run, she was unable to generate any speed because she was carrying heavy sacks of gold. Someone shouted at her to drop the moneybags, but she couldn't because they were manacled to her wrists. In another dream she was climbing a ladder that stretched to the clouds, and it began to sway dizzily. A voice that sounded like Daddy's cried, "Not high enough," so she climbed farther and farther until the ladder collapsed under her weight, and she woke with her heart pounding, her body in a cold sweat from the terror of the imaginary fall. Toward dawn she fell into another uneasy sleep, this time to dream of a curly-headed child tap-dancing to music that got faster and faster until she was stumbling in a frenzied effort to keep up the pace. Roxie woke with a dry mouth, exhausted, and climbed out of bed to brush her teeth.

All the makeup in the world isn't going to hide the damage you've done to this face, Roxie muttered to her reflection. Her eyes were puffy and bloodshot, and worst of all, they had no sparkle at all but were dull and glazed. She used some eyedrops to camouflage the streaks of red, then got some ice cubes from the freezer to shrink her swollen lids. She lay on her bed, mopping at the cold water that trickled down from the melting ice cubes, and tried to think how she could manage to live through the day. How could she go to work and face Todd? How was she to live and face herself? She massaged a gnawing ache in her abdomen and wondered if she could control her nausea. She got up and splashed more cold water on her face, then peered critically at her reflection. It didn't bear close inspection, but maybe she could get by.

She went to the closet and found a tailored black suit, its lines so severe she'd never worn it. It was exactly right for her mood today. By the time she pulled herself together and got dressed, she was an hour late for work and felt as if she were on her way to the gallows.

She tried to breeze past Lorraine but wasn't quick enough. "Roxie," called her secretary, "here, dear, I have something for you." She held out a sealed brown envelope. "Under the weather?" she asked after a careful look at Roxie's face.

"Splitting headache," Roxie mumbled. "What's this?"

"Something Todd Kendrick sent over. His secretary

was here at the stroke of eight and said you were to get it as soon as you arrived.''

Roxie felt a tightness in her throat and turned her back, hurrying to the limited safety of her own office. So Todd had decided to write a letter telling her how he despised her. Well, he was certainly entitled to do so, but she didn't think she could bear to read it. She already hated herself too much. She closed her door and eased her aching body into a chair, staring at the envelope.

The intercom buzzed. "Ready for some coffee?" asked Lorraine in her cheerful voice.

"No," Roxie answered sharply. There was a moment of silence while Lorraine recovered from her surprise. "Lorraine, I'm sorry. I've got a headache.''

"That's OK," Lorraine said, quickly forgiving. "Let me know when you're ready.''

Roxie kneaded the grooves between her eyebrows. The envelope silently mocked her from the corner of her desk. Finally she bent forward to pick it up. Might as well get it over with, she thought, ripping the seal with a long fingernail.

She removed a single sheet of paper with a few typewritten lines and a hastily scrawled signature. It took a few moments for Roxie's brain to register the typed information, and when it did, she gasped and fell back in the chair, the wind knocked from her.

The paper authorized the transfer of funds from Todd's corporate account to hers. There was no other message.

Stunned, Roxie sat staring at the paper. She had no idea how to respond to this unexpected development and was a morass of confusion. The Phoenix joint venture which yesterday seemed so urgent had lost its importance during the long, dreadful night, and her chief concern had become how to make amends to Todd and ease her own guilty conscience. This new, magnanimous gesture of Todd's only increased her guilt and made it harder for her to live with herself. Tears pricked her eyelids. She'd wanted to avoid him, but he'd given her no choice. She'd have to call and thank him. Wearily she picked up the telephone and dialed his extension.

"I'm sorry, Miss Lyons, but Mr. Kendrick has left town," said Todd's secretary. When Roxie pressed for an explanation, the secretary said he'd called her at home at 6:00 A.M. with instructions to deliver the envelope on his desk as soon as she arrived at the office.

"But where is Todd?" Roxie asked. "I need to talk to him."

"He said he was taking the early flight to Florida and wouldn't be back for several days. He didn't know where I could reach him. Can I give him a message if he happens to call in later?"

"No," Roxie said dully. "I guess it will wait until he gets back." She replaced the telephone and buzzed Lorraine on the intercom. "Come in for a minute, will you?"

By the time Lorraine entered her office, Roxie was shaking from a bad case of nerves. "Take this to the treasurer's office and have him transfer these accounts," she said, her voice trembling. "Then have him wire a draft to Phoenix to cover the joint venture levy." By the time Roxie finished giving instructions, her teeth were chattering, and Lorraine was alarmed.

"Roxie, you're ill," she said, noting the greenish hue of Roxie's complexion, her watery eyes. "Come lie down on the sofa and let me get you a wet cloth."

"Lorraine, will you please quit fussing over me and do what I asked?" Roxie cried, her irritation breaking loose. "I want this Phoenix matter taken care of immediately, do you hear me?"

"Of course," Lorraine murmured, concern in every line of her face. "Please lie down, dear, and I'll be back just as soon as I can." She snatched up the paper and hurried from the room, calling to the secretary in the next office to get a wet cloth.

By the time Lorraine returned, her mission accomplished, Roxie was stretched out on the sofa with two secretaries standing over her, one wiping her pallid face, the other massaging her temples. "Thanks," Lorraine said, dismissing them. "I can manage now. Catch my telephone for me, will you? I'm going to take her home."

"Lorraine, please, I'll be all right in a few minutes," Roxie protested, yet she was so miserable that all she could think about was getting home to bed. "I've never had a sick day in my life."

"You're having one now," Lorraine insisted. "Shall I take you home, or shall I call your father to have a look at you?"

Roxie groaned. All she needed was to have Daddy come in here, shouting and waving his arms and generally making a nuisance of himself. He'd drive her to distraction. "Oh, pooh, go ahead and take me home," she muttered ungraciously. "But I want you to know it's completely unnecessary. I'm fine, I tell you."

Lorraine didn't dream that the cause of Roxie's sickness might be a stricken conscience and therefore mistakenly diagnosed her symptoms as summer influenza. When Roxie kept trembling uncontrollably, Lorraine turned off the air conditioner and piled blankets on the bed, chafing Roxie's arms and legs to increase blood circulation. She spooned hot tea and broth down Roxie's protesting throat until eventually the hot liquid eased the chattering of her teeth. Roxie kept insisting that Lorraine return to the office, but when the chills turned to fever and Roxie began to thrash deliriously, with more eerie, tormenting dreams, she became grateful for Lorraine's comforting presence.

Throughout the day Lorraine stayed at Roxie's bedside, murmuring softly, wiping her forehead, smoothing the sheets. Toward evening Roxie's fever broke, leaving her skin ashen and clammy. "Let me brush your hair, dear, and run a damp cloth over your face. You'll feel better. I'll bring some mouthwash, too." Lorraine stepped from Roxie's bedroom to the adjoining bathroom, and when she returned, Roxie was drawn up in fetal position, sobbing. "Why, Roxie, what's wrong?" she asked in alarm. "Do you hurt somewhere?"

"I hurt all over," Roxie whispered in anguish. "You're so good to me, and I don't deserve it. I don't deserve anything from anybody." She began to rock her body back and forth. "I've never done anything but take from people, and now you're being kind, after all the times I've yelled at you." Roxie buried her head in the pillow, her shoulders shaking from the force of her sobs.

"Now, dear," Lorraine crooned, stroking Roxie's face and shoulders. "Everything is going to be all right. Please don't cry any more."

"Oh, Lorraine," Roxie wailed, lifting her head and throwing herself into Lorraine's arms. "I'm so ashamed of myself. What am I going to do?" She clutched Lorraine's neck and cried inconsolably, her tears soaking the front of Lorraine's blouse, while Lorraine stroked her long tresses and murmured words of comfort.

"You don't understand," Roxie said brokenly. "What I did was terrible. I'll never be able to forgive myself, never."

Lorraine held her tight and let her cry herself out. She now realized that whatever was wrong with Roxie, it was emotional, not physical, and she didn't want to pry into a personal matter of such magnitude that it had reduced her high-flying Roxie to a cowering heap. Eventually Roxie cried herself to a state of exhaustion and fell asleep in Lorraine's arms. When Lorraine lowered her tousled head to the pillow and started to slip away, Roxie roused enough to whisper, "Please, don't leave me."

"I'll be right here, dear," Lorraine responded, and settled down in a floral chintz chair to wait out the night. When she was sure Roxie was sleeping deeply, Lorraine tiptoed out and made a quick telephone call to George Lyons to let him know that Roxie was much improved and would soon be on the mend. She then fixed herself a quick bite to eat and returned to the bedroom upstairs, glad to see that Roxie was now sprawled on the brass bed, one arm across her face, rather than curled up in a tight ball. Lorraine leaned back in the chair and tried to doze.

Toward dawn she heard Roxie call her name. "I'm right here, Roxie. Do you need something?"

"I'd like to talk to you," Roxie said in a despair-laden voice. "I've got to talk to somebody or I'm going to go crazy." It was the time of night when darkness provides an intimacy and permits conversations that are impossible in the harsher light of day. Thus with her face hidden in protective shadows, Roxie was able to tell Lorraine things she'd never have been able to say otherwise; in a voice that faltered and often broke completely, she told Lorraine the whole sordid story.

Lorraine shared Roxie's anguish but didn't pass judgment on her. When Roxie had finished the tale, Lorraine asked only one question. "Do you know why you did it, Roxie?"

"Because I wanted my division to be first so Daddy would be proud of me. I want him to know I'm better than his best employee."

"But, Roxie, your father *is* proud of you, you know that."

"Oh, he's proud of me because I'm cute and because I wear pretty clothes. He's proud of me because I have fetching ways and have a trail of men following me. But he's never been proud of me as a person or of my work, no matter what I've done. I thought this time I could finally get his attention."

Lorraine sighed and thought of the man she'd known and admired for so many years. George was bigger than life, one of those people whose personality is overwhelming and influences others disproportionately. He was a good man in many ways, but Lorraine had spotted his feet of clay early on and was realistic about his faults. Poor Roxie had seen only the towering giant. "Roxie," she said softly, "I've known your father a long time. I've worked for him for more than thirty years, since before you were born. I'm very fond of him. But I've watched you all these years, trying so hard to be just like him, when all he ever wanted was for you to be his baby girl, all dressed up for a dance recital so he could sit in the front row and show off how pretty you were."

Roxie exhaled a shaky breath. "That was okay when I was a little girl, but I'm a grown woman, now. I want him to be proud of what I am and what I can do, not what I look like."

"And you think if you can make yourself into the spitting image of him, you'll finally get that approval he's held back from you?"

Roxie shook her head. "I just don't know any more. But I thought I had to try." She sat up in bed and propped a pillow on her bent knees, then burrowed her head in it. "But look what happened. In trying to make Daddy proud, I made myself ashamed."

"Roxie, you're going to have to try to understand your father. He started his company at the end of World War II when the country was in a state of economic turmoil. The only way to be successful was to be ruthless, and for men in his generation, the only thing that mattered was success. Your dad's company survived two more wars and no telling how many recessions because he was tough and willing to sacrifice everything to get to the top. But it did something to him, and there's a streak of cruelty and callousness in him now that wasn't there when he was young." Lorraine paused, her mind drifting back in time, thinking of George as a young man, enthusiastic and virile. "I think he knows it changed him. All he has left of that eager young man is you, Roxie. And he's tried to hold onto that part of himself by keeping you a baby, at least in his own mind. He can't let himself admit you've grown up . . . and grown up to be just like him. So he ignores everything you do at work because he despises the dark side of his own character."

There was a long silence while each woman was lost in her own thoughts. "But what am I going to do?" Roxie said at last, her voice trembling in the silence. "I can't go on being a cute little girl just because that's what Daddy wants from me. I've grown up, whether he likes it or not, and I have to make my life count for something."

"Yes, you've grown up . . . in some ways. But part of you is still like a little girl at her dance recital, waiting for Daddy to applaud. Everything you do is designed to get his attention, and when you can't get it from him, you look for approval from other men. Isn't that why you flirt with every man in sight?"

"I never thought about it. I just did it because it was fun. I like having men admire me and fuss over me." She lifted her head, startled. "Just like Daddy did when I was a little girl!"

Lorraine wanted to help Roxie reach the truth about herself and thereby be freed from bondage to the past. "Who's the only man you ever met who didn't approve of you?"

"Todd Kendrick," Roxie said. "He detests me. For good reason." She flopped on her stomach and pulled the pillow over her head, trying to muffle her tears in the mattress.

Lorraine patted her shoulder, knowing these were cleansing tears that would bring relief. "It's almost seven o'clock, Roxie. I'm going to call your dad and tell him you're still weak and need another day in bed. And then I'm going to take a day off myself. I think I need a good nap." She smiled, thinking of the way George would bellow when she told him. But she'd never taken a day off in thirty years unless he was out of the office, too. It would be good for him to manage without her for one day. "Call me at home if you need anything," she said, softly closing the door behind her. But Roxie was already asleep.

For the first time in her life, Roxie was drained of energy and finally returned to work two days later drawn and listless. She gave exaggerated accounts of her bout of "influenza" to explain her wan complexion and fatigue and spent most of her time secluded in her office staring out the window at the Dallas skyline. She learned the following week that Todd had returned from his trip, and she tried several times to call him. When his secretary continued to say that he was away from his desk, Roxie concluded that he was avoiding her and abandoned her efforts. It was just as well. She still didn't know what she could possibly say that would erase the memory of what she'd done to him.

As July wore on, so did her nerves, and she found it increasingly difficult to make small talk and to be her usual vivacious, charming self. Julian and Rusty would seek her out from time to time, reporting their latest financial exploits, and she found their company both tiresome and juvenile. Though she did her best to give the smiling encouragement they expected from her, it now came through gritted teeth. She became extremely bored with their braggadocio about the contest and irritated that they treated her like the prize in a box of Cracker Jacks. The thought of marrying either of them made her nauseated. When she could bear it no longer, she propelled herself into her father's office.

"Daddy, we've got to call off this stupid contest," she said without preliminaries, surprising him so much he almost dropped his coffee mug. "It's the worst idea I ever had in my life."

"Why, Roxie," he sputtered, "how can you say that? Profits are up, up, up, zooming through the roof. There's nothing like the right motivation to get the hired help running on the old treadmill."

"Daddy, listen to me," she said, biting off her words. "I said it isn't going to work. I can't marry one of those guys just because he made a lot of money for you."

"Why, sure you can. You love both of them already, you know you do."

"Both of them?"

"Julian and Rusty. I don't know which one will win, but they're both fine boys."

"What about Todd? He was ahead last month."

"Just a temporary aberration. He hasn't done a

damn thing this month. No, it'll be either Julian or Rusty."

"Daddy, I don't love them. I'll never love them. And I won't marry either one of them."

George put down the financial spreadsheet in his hand and glowered at her. "What do you mean you won't marry either one of them? By God, Roxie, we gave our word. You can't back out on me now. It's too late."

"Don't tell me it's too late," Roxie said, nervously twisting her ring. It was so hard to stand up to Daddy. He just wouldn't listen to anything he didn't agree with. "Business isn't everything, Daddy. We're talking about my future. I can't marry someone I don't love."

George snorted with derisive laughter. "Love, baloney. You know better than to blubber about that kind of nonsense."

"You're the one who told me to fall in love first and then get married, just like you and Mama did."

"Roxie, you know very good and well that your mama and I hardly knew each other when we got married. She had four sections of land I wanted, and I owned a downtown office building her papa wanted. And do you know something? We fell in love just like they do in the movies. You know why, Roxie? Because you can fall in love with anybody. All you have to do is set your mind to it."

"Don't count on it," Roxie said, her arms stiff at her sides. "I warn you, Daddy. I'm not going to let myself be raffled off to the highest bidder."

"Sit yourself down, young lady, and listen to me." George's face was turning purplish with outrage. He didn't allow anybody to cross him, not even Roxie. She sat down and glared at him. "I gave you a chance in the beginning to wait until you fell in love, but you said it didn't matter. Told me some crazy story about those IQ tests at the bank and how they proved you'd never fall in love or something. So I called in my men, and I sold them on your idea . . . *your* idea, Roxie, not mine. And they've been busting their butts for four months, now, accomplishing one miracle after another. And now you think you're going to bounce in here and tell me you've changed your mind? You think I'm going back to my boys after all they've done and say the deal is off? You're nuts, Roxie. I'd never be able to hold up my head in this company again. I'd have to sell out."

"You'd never be able to hold up *your* head? Is that all you can think about, Daddy? Yourself? What about me? Don't my feelings make any difference?" She was so angry that her voice was shaking, but George was too consumed with his own temper to pay any heed.

"I love you more than anything in life, Roxie, but I won't let you destroy my company."

"Then you love the company more than you do me."

"Stop twisting things around. You know that's not true." George suddenly realized that they were shouting at each other. "Roxie, sweetheart," he said, getting up and going over to her chair, sinking beside her and pulling her against his burly chest, "you're just tired, princess. You've been working too hard, you've been sick, it's all the excitement catching up with you." He stroked her soft hair, genuinely concerned, genuinely affectionate. "You're my precious baby girl, Roxie. I don't want you to be unhappy, sweetheart."

"Oh, Daddy," she cried, leaning against him while salty tears dripped down her cheeks. "I've never been so unhappy in my whole life. What am I going to do?"

He took her delicate face between his big, rough hands and wiped her tears with his thumbs. George was tough as bullhide and could handle anything life had to dish out except his daughter's tears. "Hell, sweetheart, we'll just have to figure out something else. Give me a few days and I'll come up with something." He took his handkerchief from his pocket and wiped her tears. "Don't cry, baby. Leave it to your old daddy. I'll fix it for you."

She hiccoughed against him. "I'm not a little girl any more, Daddy. You can't fix this the way you used to fix my roller skates and my doll."

George felt a wrenching sensation that squeezed his lungs and made it hard to breathe. What was the world coming to if a man couldn't protect his own sweet baby girl? He passed a hand over his lined cheeks and realized that he was getting old. But surely he was still wily enough to fix things and make Roxie happy again. "I love you, princess," he said, hugging her against his chest.

"Oh, Daddy, I love you, too." She clung to his neck for a moment of comfort, then stole a look at his face. "Are you disappointed in me?" she asked.

"Never you mind about that," he said, refusing to meet her eye. "What matters is that my baby girl is happy again." He got to his feet, his knee joints creaking, and walked to the window, carefully keeping his back to her so she wouldn't be able to read his expression. How could he help but be disappointed? But that didn't matter, he had to fix things for his baby and get that smile back on her face before she broke his heart. "Tell you what," he said, staring at the fluffy white clouds floating on the skyline. "Why don't you take a long weekend and go up to the company lodge at Lake Texoma for a few days? It's nice and peaceful there, and you can think things over."

"Daddy, please, I *have* thought things over," Roxie protested.

"Who knows, you might change your mind once you've had a good rest."

George was so determined that it was hard to dissuade him from an idea, but Roxie made one last effort. "Daddy, let's worry about it later, OK?"

"Sure thing, princess. We'll worry about it *after* you've taken yourself a nice, long weekend. One way or another, I'm going to see those happy dimples come back in my baby's cheeks."

He turned to face her, trying to smile reassuringly, but the troubled expression in his eyes made her feel guilty. She was a grown woman and needed to solve her own problems instead of dumping them on her father.

"Daddy, I can't go to the lake. I have work to do."

"Never mind about your work. I can handle anything that comes up." He paused, reflecting. The best thing was to get Roxie out of the office while the fur was flying. Everybody was running neck and neck in the contest and business was booming. No wonder Roxie was distraught. There was so much tension in the office that everybody was infected with it. Even

Lorraine had snapped at him yesterday, for the first time in thirty years. "You go home and pack your bathing suit and pick up a few fresh fruits and vegetables. Everything else is already stocked." Before Roxie quite realized what had happened, her father was shooing her out of the office. She tried to resist, but when he insisted, she didn't have the energy to argue any more.

She was almost to the elevator when she realized that there was one task that nobody, not even George, could do for her. She hurried back to her desk and hastily scrawled a note to Todd. "Please forgive me," it said. "And thank you for saving my skin with the transfer of funds. I wouldn't have been so generous if I'd been in your shoes." After handing the note to Lorraine with instructions to be sure that Todd read it, Roxie went home to pack. Before she got to North Central Expressway, George already had his head burrowed into the latest financial projections. The month would end tomorrow, and it looked like the profits for July would go down in history.

Chapter Eight

*R*oxie made her way through the usual traffic snarls on North Central Expressway and had to give all her attention to maneuvering her Porsche without mishap. Once she passed the huge North Park shopping center the traffic eased somewhat, and by the time she got to Richardson it had thinned to the point where she could simultaneously increase her speed and decrease her concentration. Long before she got to the cutoff at Denison and headed the car toward Lake Texoma, her mind was totally absorbed in the conversation she'd had with her father.

If only she could find a way to fix this mess she'd gotten herself into! Of course Daddy would be embarrassed; she'd put him in a terrible position. And he'd grumble about it from now on. Roxie remembered with painful clarity his long memory for other people's mistakes and wondered momentarily if it were worth it. Maybe she ought to go on as if nothing had happened, marry the winner of the contest as originally planned, and live happily ever after. Which would be harder for her, to listen to Daddy complain and know he'd never have any confidence in her again, or to spend the rest of her life manufacturing smiles and billing and cooing like some retarded turtle dove? She'd played the role of Daddy's darling so long it had become second nature. What would it cost her to add another role to her repertory and play Julian's darling, or Rusty's darling? Or Todd's darling? . . .

She grimaced and pulled through a gate, then wound past the many cottages and lodges nestled in the trees until she reached the contemporary-styled lodge of soaring glass and cedar that belonged to Sunshine Enterprises. The long, deep lake reflected the brilliant blue of the sky, and a slight breeze riffled waves with tiny caps of white foam. It was lovely here, a welcome retreat from the bustle and noise of the city. There was no point in driving herself crazy stewing about the contest. She was so mixed up right now she couldn't think clearly. She eyed the beckoning lake.

I'm just going to go jump in the water and let it carry me as far as it'll go. Maybe tomorrow I'll wake up in Oklahoma and find out this is nothing but a bad dream. She grabbed her small travel bag and the paper sack of fruits and vegetables and hurried to unlock the door.

The lodge was spacious, with the ceiling of the main room soaring twenty feet to an open-beamed ceiling of satin-smooth cedar. A fireplace of native stone dominated one wall and had a hand-woven rug in front of it. There were many comfortable chairs and several couches, large and small, because the lodge was often used for company planning meetings and could accommodate a crowd. There were two nice-sized bedrooms with private baths, plus another large dormitory-style room with bunk beds and a latrine for the male-dominated company fishing trips. Adjacent to the massive central room was a dining area with a long trestle table and a smaller round table, and behind the wall was a well-equipped kitchen complete with microwave oven, dishwasher and ice maker. The exterior wall was entirely glass and opened onto a redwood deck with more dining tables, lounge chairs and a brick barbecue pit.

Roxie went into the kitchen and put milk, eggs, lettuce, tomatoes, carrots, mushrooms, peaches, plums and oranges in the refrigerator, then removed a package of chopped sirloin from the freezer to thaw. Maybe tomorrow she would feel like eating something and could grill a meat patty on the barbecue pit. For tonight she'd settle for a salad and a boiled egg with her iced tea.

She took her travel bag into one of the bedrooms and unpacked it, strewing clothes over the woven plaid bedspread and tossing some of them in a drawer of the maple dresser. Like the rest of the lodge, the bedroom was simply decorated but comfortable. Even with a caretaker, George was too practical to tempt thieves by placing expensive furnishings in an often-vacant lodge. Roxie hung her robe and extra slacks in the closet, then stripped off her clothes and got into her bathing suit, a cobalt blue bikini that barely covered the essentials. She got her sunglasses and a towel, prowled around until she found a tube of tanning lotion, and headed through the trees toward the lake.

The beach was reasonably uncrowded, since it was a weekday, and she had all the privacy she wanted as she stretched out on her towel, digging her toes into the sand. The late afternoon sun seemed unusually hot, and she squirmed under its rays, estimating the time as carefully as she could and turning regularly to keep from scorching her delicate skin. After thirty minutes she went into the water, cool and refreshing on her perspiring body. She floated lazily, letting the water carry her cares away, at least for the moment, while she delighted in the lap of the waves against her face. Time after time she ducked her head, then came up splashing and spitting water like a child. For once in his life Daddy had the right idea, she thought, enjoying the solitude, the play of water against her skin.

She did a somersault in the water, then swam with long, easy strokes toward sailboats skimming along the horizon. A motorboat pulling a water-skier cut past, churning up a foaming wake in its path. The driver, a bronzed, healthy male, waved jauntily and cut a circle around Roxie, momentarily imprisoning her within a ring of waves. She laughed at his antics and waved back, noting the scowl on the pretty face of his female passenger until he zoomed on. She treaded water until the waves calmed, then swam back toward shore.

Her body felt blissfully weary, and by the time she'd taken a shower and changed into her shorts, she was ravenously hungry. She made a huge salad, ate two boiled eggs and half a dozen crackers, then yielded to temptation and ate one of the ice cream bars she found in the freezer. She flipped the dial on the television set and sank down on the hand-woven rug, a pillow at her back, to watch the summer rerun of a less-than-sparkling comedy program. Long before Johnny Carson started his monologue, Roxie was sound asleep, sprawled on her stomach with one arm wrapped around the pillow. For the first time in weeks she was freed from the dreams that had haunted her and snored with the untroubled sleep of a child.

She woke to the song of a meadowlark in the tall cedar tree outside the picture window and eased to her feet, stretching her protesting muscles. Stiff from her night on the floor yet curiously refreshed, Roxie made herself a cup of instant coffee in the microwave and carried it with her to the beach. She took a long walk to loosen her joints and discovered a group of college students picnicking in a nearby cove. She stopped to chat with them and felt her spirits lift with their enthusiastic high jinks. One clean-shaven young man was trying unsuccessfully to fish from the bank, so Roxie offered the use of the company motorboat. The students seized upon the opportunity and followed Roxie back down the beach to the boathouse and helped her push out the boat, then start it up. They all climbed aboard its thirty-foot length, several of them making use of the flyrods and tackle after the boat slowly idled its way to the center of the lake and they dropped anchor.

Roxie sat in one corner of the cabin and listened to

their entertaining tales of college life. They seemed so very young to her, so fresh and innocent. Had she been like that at their age? She tried to remember her own college days at Stanford, but it seemed that even then she'd been caught up in the compulsion to succeed. No doubt she'd spent some time at the ocean, but had she ever relaxed as these kids were doing? She didn't remember ever before in her life having a carefree day like this.

They caught an abundance of bass and perch, and by noon the sun was so hot that they were eager to return to shore and cook their catch. Roxie dropped the group at their campsite before returning the boat to the dock, but accepted their sincere invitation to join them for lunch. She walked back down the beach with the sun beating on her shoulders, her mind drifting as aimlessly as a cork in the water. Usually she was so wired up and nervous from a heavy workload and too much caffeine that it was foreign to her to let herself unwind peacefully like this. Now that she had stopped the flow of adrenaline, she wondered if she could ever get charged up again. She felt as limp as a rag doll, completely lethargic.

The fresh air enhanced her appetite, and she enjoyed a hearty meal with her beach mates, eating such a quantity of grilled fish and campfire potatoes that she thought she might burst. The air rang with laughter and music from a portable radio, and Roxie was a receptive audience for increasingly outrageous tales of college exploits. As the afternoon lengthened, however, she noticed that the group was beginning to pair off, the couples more absorbed in each other than with the group. Feeling like a fifth wheel, she bade them good-bye and wandered back down the beach to her own spot, now quiet and lonely after the camaraderie of the day.

Thinking she might take it out for a ride, she dragged the company's canoe from the boathouse to the beach. By then she was drenched with sweat and decided it was too hot for the exertion of paddling the canoe, so she beached it in a tall, deserted cove and went for a swim instead.

She hadn't been in the water long before she saw a tall figure running down the beach, stopping occasionally to scan the water with one hand over his eyes. Just as she recognized the figure as Todd's, she heard his voice echo across the water, calling her name. She shouted at him, but the wind carried her voice back across the water and he couldn't hear her. Wondering why he'd come and feeling a sudden excitement, she started swimming toward shore.

He saw her before she reached him and stood waiting, his hands on his hips, while she drew herself out of the water and stood dripping in front of him.

"Hello," she said, churning with a sudden shyness. She hadn't seen him or talked to him in a month, since the night . . .

"I was afraid something had happened to you," he said, embarrassed at his panic when he hadn't been able to find her. "Your dad sent me up here, and when I couldn't find you in the lodge, I noticed the canoe was gone. I ran all down the beach, but there were only sailboats and motorboats." He realized that he was talking too fast and broke off abruptly.

"The canoe is over in that cove," she said, pointing. "I decided I was too tired to paddle it by myself, so I went swimming instead."

"Tired? You?" he asked in surprise. She was always so disgustingly full of energy.

She shrugged. "I haven't been feeling too well lately."

"That's what your dad told me when he asked me to come up here."

They both became intensely interested in the sand at their feet.

"Is he checking up on his baby girl?" Roxie asked at last to break the silence. "I didn't mean to worry him."

"No, it wasn't that," Todd answered. "He wanted me to bring you the preliminary financial reports for July. He had one of those weird ideas he gets sometimes that it would cheer you up to see last month's profits. They went through the ceiling, of course."

Roxie scuffed the sand with her bare foot. At the moment, with Todd standing before her, his expression inscrutable, she had no interest whatsoever in the company's profits. That could wait. What mattered now was finding some way to express her apologies to Todd for what she'd done to him. "Todd," she whispered, and looked up.

He was waiting for her to continue, his head cocked at an angle. Positioned as they were, with Roxie standing at the edge of the beach and Todd on the slope above her, he towered over her. His head blocked out the sun, so that his body was silhouetted against the sand dunes. He looked as solid as granite and as unmoving.

Catching him by surprise and knocking the wind out of him, Roxie yielded to an irresistible impulse to throw herself into his arms.

"Todd, I don't know what to say," she wailed, burying her face in his neck and clinging to him for dear life. "I'm so sorry and so ashamed of myself and I know you'll never be able to forgive me, but I've learned my lesson, I promise. Please don't hate me, Todd, please. I can't bear it if you go on hating me," she whispered.

Todd put his arms around her and drew her close against him while her tears soaked the front of his shirt. He rocked her back and forth, his gentle hands brushing the hair from her eyes. He'd hated her with a consuming passion for the past month, but now he was genuinely touched. Or was it all an act? He put his hands around her face and pushed it slightly away from him, wondering whether she was trying to deceive him again. "I've never seen you without all that makeup before," he said in surprise as he got a good look at her face. "I didn't know you were so beautiful."

Beautiful? With her nose red and runny, her face wrinkled with tears, and not even one dab of mascara? She collapsed against him, hysterical with laughter and tears, her body shaking uncontrollably. "I'm ruining your shirt," she said, her words muffled against his warm, muscular chest.

"For shame," he whispered. He removed his hands from her back and unbuttoned his shirt, tossing it on the sand at their feet. "Now you can come back," he said, pulling her against the strength of his body. "Don't cry any more, Roxie," he crooned against her hair, brushing it with his lips. "Let's just forget it and start all over, OK?"

Roxie wiped her eyes with one hand and brushed the tears against her damp bathing suit. "It seems like we're always having to start over."

"That's because we're always getting off on the wrong foot. Maybe it will be different this time." He held her head away from him and gazed deeply into her eyes, searching for the inner person she always tried to hide. "I've said some pretty nasty things myself. Will you forgive me if I'll forgive you?"

She nodded, feeling a wonderful release from her guilt.

"Friends?" he asked.

"Friends," she said gratefully, offering her hand for him to shake. When she lifted her eyes, he was smiling at her. "Oh, Todd, you're the most handsome man in the world when you smile like that," she said, suddenly breathless.

"Watch the flattery," he scolded, lightly swatting her fanny. "A man in my condition is too susceptible to female wiles." He'd come up here on business, and only at George's shouted insistence. He wasn't about to leave himself wide open for a repetition of his last two encounters with Roxie Lyons. This frustrated, demanding body of his couldn't take any more provocation. "Let's go up to the lodge, and I'll give you the financial reports. I left them on the dining table."

"Screw the damned financial reports," Roxie muttered, catching his hand and holding it against her rounded hip.

Todd lifted an eyebrow in surprise. It wasn't like Roxie to turn a cold shoulder to financial matters, not at all. *Down boy,* he grumbled to himself. Surely you've learned by now not to get your hopes up. "Did you have something else in mind?" he asked softly.

She lifted her face and gazed into Todd's eyes. All her flirtatious banter was gone now, replaced by a diffident tenderness. The sun was dropping to the western horizon, bathing the sky in a splendor of red and orange, trailing to soft pink at the edges. "I thought we might go out in the canoe and watch the sunset," she whispered. "That's something I've never done in my whole life, and tonight seems like a good time to start."

Todd held her against his chest. "You have to sit awfully still in a canoe or else it'll tip over," he said, pondering the situation.

"There are lots of extra bathing trunks at the lodge," Roxie replied. "Just in case you happen to get wet."

"I'll be right back. Or would you like to go with me?"

Roxie hugged her arms around herself. "No," she said shyly. "If I do, we might not make it back in time to see the sunset, and that's something I'd especially like to share with you. My very first sunset."

There was a constriction in Todd's throat and he swallowed hard. "Can't think of anything I'd enjoy more," he said, hurrying to the lodge.

When he returned they paddled the canoe to the center of the lake and watched the boats skim gracefully across the water, their sails taut against the breeze. From time to time a motorboat whirred past, sending out ripples that gently rocked the canoe. The blue sky deepened to lavender, then purple, its darkening reflection turning the water a swirling indigo. The soft shadows of twilight cast a hush across the lake, and Roxie and Todd sat in the swaying canoe, their hands linked, without speaking. The flaming fireball that was the sun swept to its western grave in a blaze of glory, setting the sky aflame as it passionately ended the day.

"Isn't that a beautiful sunset?" Roxie murmured, pressing Todd's hand. "Words don't even do it justice, it's so breathtaking."

He returned the pressure of her hand and nodded. There was no need to speak.

At the precise moment the sun dipped below the horizon, leaving the sky a lonely midnight-blue, Todd leaned forward to kiss Roxie and capsized the canoe.

"Todd, you did that on purpose," she cried, laughing as she splashed in the water. Her swimsuit was quickly soaked and clung to the enticing curves of her body. She pushed her soggy hair back from her face with both hands, treading water to stay afloat.

"I didn't plan it quite like that," he answered from the other side of the overturned canoe. "I thought I'd get my kiss first. I intended to give you a thrilling end to your first sunset." He flipped the canoe topside, the muscles bulging in his arms and shoulders. "Where are you?" he asked. "I can't find you in the dark."

Roxie swam around the boat and drew up behind Todd, putting one arm around his waist and hugging against him while she kept herself afloat with the other arm. "I'm right here," she whispered against his cheek.

"So I notice." His free arm stroked her bare legs as they floated in the water, then pulled them against him and locked them around his own. Her lips trailed kisses across his wet shoulders, then buried themselves in his neck. It was exciting to feel the tiny goosebumps rise on his skin at her touch, and she wondered why she'd never experienced this kind of erotic pleasure before. She let her head fall back into the water, cool against her scalp, and felt as though she were being reborn, quickened and alive sexually in a way she'd never known.

Her hand caressed the warm skin of Todd's chest, traced lazy circles from his collarbone to the waistband of his swimsuit. She felt his muscles tighten as her fingers darted downward, below the cool water, but he couldn't control the involuntary reaction of his body to her touch. She knew a woman's secret sense of power when his manhood sprang to life under her fingers, and her heart raced to think how much she wanted to pleasure him with her body.

"Roxie," he groaned, searching for her mouth, twisting in an urgent effort to bring their straining bodies closer together.

"Ummm," she murmured from behind him, playfully nipping his ear.

He sharply drew in his breath, intoxicated with her nearness, and fumbled for the soft warmth of her breasts. "Roxie, please," he whispered brokenly, "let me make love to you. Please, darling, don't make me wait any longer, not when I want you so much."

His words fell on the gentle waves like music, mesmerizing Roxie. She lifted her torso and yanked the string to her bikini top, then removed it and tossed it in the bottom of the canoe. She lowered her bare breasts against his back with short, sensuous strokes, then twisted her body and dived underwater, emerging just out of his reach. The fading light cast shadows, bathing the globes of her breasts a translucent white that darkened at the tips.

"So this is what a sea nymph looks like," Todd said, bewitched by her beauty. He swam toward her and locked his arms around her, burying his face against her wet skin while he breathed the fragrance of her hair. He lifted his head and gazed at her, then lowered his mouth to hers.

His kiss was tender at first, but as their bodies clung together he felt a rising excitement and probed her willing mouth with his eager tongue. They tred water faster and faster, partly to stay afloat and partly because the quickened rhythm matched their quickened pulsebeat. When they drew apart to take rapid, shallow breaths, Todd swam to the canoe and turned to face Roxie as she drew up beside him.

"Put your arms around me and hold onto the canoe," he said. "It'll hold you up."

"What's going to hold you up?" she asked.

"You are," he said with a wicked grin.

Roxie followed his instructions, circling him within her arms while her body supported him, leaving his own hands free. "Todd," she gasped, when she realized what he had in mind. "Somebody will see us."

"It's almost dark. Besides, you didn't worry about that when you took off your top," he replied.

"Nobody was close enough to see me," she insisted.

"There's nobody close to us now," he said. "So come here, you little daredevil, and let's see if we can't heat up this water before we freeze to death."

His arms locked around her while he sweetly plundered her mouth again and again until she was dizzy with desire. When she moaned softly, her head leaning on his shoulder, his hands reached out to fondle and caress her breasts, their nipples already puckered from the stimulation provided by the water. She tried to hoist herself in the water to get closer to him, but the canoe started to tip and she quickly righted herself.

"Let me manage this," he said, and lowered his own body in the darkened water, still imprisoned between her arms and the canoe. In one graceful movement he ducked his head and sought her waiting breast, teasing its nipple to a throbbing readiness. Her breath came faster, and he turned to the other breast with an exciting suction. Roxie wanted to let go of the canoe and rake her fingernails across his back, to clutch him in frenzied response, but she didn't dare. All she could do was thrust against him and moan with pleasure.

His hands slipped below the water and loosened the drawstring on her bikini bottom, then tugged it loose and tossed it over his head into the canoe. When he'd done the same thing with his own swim trunks, he slid his body against Roxie's, slick in the water. She exulted in their nakedness, straining against him as his hands ignited her to an unquenchable flame. She didn't resist when his fingers made their way to the throbbing center of her being, knowing that only he could ease the sweet aching she felt there. He stroked her to a pulsing, insistent readiness, then gripped her hips with his hands and lowered her body onto his, thrusting himself inside her with shock waves of desire. Again and again he plunged into her, his voracious lunges sending ripples across the surface of the lake.

Roxie sought his mouth, pushing his head against the canoe as she thrust her tongue to meet his in a thrilling duet. Todd's wet hands clasped her breasts, fondling them until frothy waves lapped at her skin. He tore his mouth from hers to suck greedily at her breasts, then with a hoarse cry jerked her head backward and relentlessly plundered her mouth until spasms exploded inside her. Todd shuddered, then surrendered to the same spasms, and they plunged together into a tidal wave of desire, paradoxically drowning in it yet at the same time riding its crest to triumphant release. . . .

"Is that what it's like to drown?" Roxie asked dreamily when her body had quit trembling.

Todd kissed her cheek and lifted her nude body into the canoe, then climbed in beside her. "Nope. Nothing else on earth can be that sweet," he answered softly. "Have we lost a paddle?" he asked, spotting only one.

The lake and sky had melded to a solid blue black, and if a paddle floated in the darkness, it was impossible to see it. "Guess I won't be able to help you, then," Roxie said, laughing softly. "Besides, my arms are tired from hanging onto the boat."

"When we get back I'll massage your shoulders," Todd said, turning the canoe toward shore with long, smooth strokes of the paddle. They drifted in silence, still caught up in the rapture of the moment, their bodies tingling with the memory of their lovemaking. The gulls were silent now, and there was no sound except the echo of the paddle strokes against the water. By good fortune, no other boats crossed their path, and they experienced their own private Eden, secure from prying eyes but free to gaze at each other's bodies, now luminous in the moonlight.

By the time they reached shore their desire had rekindled, and Todd beached the canoe in the same hidden cove, then lowered Roxie onto the towel she'd left behind. They scattered the sand as they tumbled over and over, their eager bodies locked together, thrusting and yielding. Passion catapulted them to the furthest edge of rapture, then beyond, until they were suspended, trembling, in a paradise of their own creation. With a hoarse cry, they collapsed in each other's arms, exhausted and radiant.

Chapter Nine

The moon was high in the heavens, bathing the dunes and water with translucent beauty, when Todd shifted in his sleep and felt the sand underneath him. Remembering, he blinked his eyes and found Roxie snuggled into a ball beside him, her hair drifting across his chest. For a long time he gazed down at her sleeping form, his head propped on one elbow, and felt a strange tenderness toward her. She looked so vulnerable now, so open and trusting. He leaned forward and brushed her lips, then scooped her in his arms and carried her across the hundred yards of beach to the lodge. She opened her eyes once and smiled at him, then lay her head on his shoulder with a sigh and fell back asleep. Pulling back the covers with one hand, he lowered her into the bed and crawled in beside her, enjoying the feel of her naked body close against his. His hand played over her silky skin, his lips brushed her hair and cheek, and one time he called her name. She was sleeping too soundly to hear him, though, so he sheltered her in his arms and commanded his yearning body to wait until morning.

Roxie was first to hear the song of the meadowlark as it wakened the sleeping world. She awoke happy, not knowing why until memory caught up with consciousness and she felt the warm strength of Todd's arms around her. She shifted to face him and ran her fingernail with a soft rasp across the stubble on his cheeks. His eyes instantly flew open, their gold flecks dancing. "God, but you're beautiful with lake weeds in your hair," he whispered, pulling her face toward him so he could kiss her good morning. "I thought you'd never wake up."

Roxie briefly considered reminding him that she'd been the first to wake, but he was kissing her so deliciously that she didn't have breath to argue. Her hands delighted in the ripple of muscles under his skin, and a sensitive fingertip found marks on his back. "What happened to you?" she asked, lifting her head to peek over his shoulder.

"I think I tangled with a wildcat last night." He laughed softly at the memory of her fingernails raking his back as they tumbled across the dune in a passionate embrace.

Roxie pushed Todd onto his stomach and began to kiss the red streaks and welts. "Feel better?" she murmured against his back, her breath a caress.

"Not yet," he said, scarcely moving as her tongue and lips played across his skin, raising little pleasure bumps. Her fingers traveled down the bony ridges of his spine, tracing circles, and her lips followed to kiss them away. She felt him stiffen when her lips reached the base of his spine, and she laughed, then moved her mouth to the soft skin between his rib cage and his hip bone, blowing and tickling until he twisted underneath her and wrapped his arms around his sides to evade her torment. "Roxie, stop it," he cried, tears watering his eyes. "I'm ticklish. I can't stand any more."

"Oh, well, in that case," she said with a pout, trailing her fingers down his hip, across to his belly button, then darting playfully across his springy mat of hair before removing her hands and clasping them behind her back. "In that case, I guess we might as well get up."

Todd reached behind her and unclasped her hands, then brought them back to their original location, where he'd sprung to life and throbbed at her touch. He buried his face in her neck, kissing her in a way that made her melt with desire. "In that case," he said gruffly, "I don't know why you're in such a rush. This is Saturday, remember? We can stay in bed as long as we want."

He kissed her so hungrily that he almost didn't hear her breathless whisper, "Oh, Todd, I want."

It was mid-morning when they woke again, temporarily sated and glowing from their lovemaking. Drowsily they crawled out of bed, showered together and tugged on their bathing suits, their hands and lips frequently caressing and clinging as though they were bereft when apart. They wondered why they were so hungry until they remembered that they'd had no dinner the night before, so they cooked a big breakfast, sharing the tasks and feeding each other bites as they worked. They took their food out on the deck and stretched out on lounge chairs to enjoy the warmth of the sun on their skin while they munched crispy bacon and toast and sipped fresh-perked coffee. They talked about nothing in particular, laughing often, and Todd thought that Roxie's laughter must be the most enchanting sound on earth. He bent his elbows and folded his hands under his head, thinking up one amusing story after another so he could listen to her laugh.

"You've changed so much," she said with a sense of wonder. "You never used to be any fun. I think I knew you six months before I ever saw you smile."

"You've changed yourself," he answered. "You were such a barracuda I couldn't trust you long enough to turn my back."

She chuckled. "Actually, I think I'm more interested in your front. Though I have to say, you do have a pretty nice—"

"Roxie Lyons!" he gasped in mock horror. "Watch your mouth or I'll wash it out with soap."

She picked up the tube of tanning lotion and sent it sailing across the porch in his direction. "If you do, you'll never find out what I have in mind for our afternoon nap."

A luscious prickle crept through Todd. Roxie was full of surprises, as unpredictable as a child—but also a very sensual woman. He leaned back with a smile. He could hardly wait to find out what she was planning.

They talked idly for a while longer until the conversation inevitably turned to the office and business. "I've never seen George so excited," Todd said, remembering how Roxie's father had caught him returning from a trip to Houston after everyone else had left for the day. "He insisted that I drop everything and bring the new financial reports to you. He seemed to think you couldn't live another hour without knowing the company had broken all past earnings records."

Roxie swallowed the last sip of her orange juice. "He's proud of the company and the way everyone is working so hard," she said, her voice thoughtful. "And he counts on me to feel the same way about it. I always have, you know."

Todd's grin lit up his face. "Isn't that the way all men are, showing off for their females? What good does it do to build a profitable company if there's not someone there to cheer your performance?"

Roxie tilted her head, thinking. Is that what Daddy was doing, waiting for her to applaud his performance? When all the time she was waiting for *him* to applaud *hers?* But neither one of them seemed to applaud at the right time. Daddy applauded her when she looked pretty, and she applauded him when . . . when he took care of her and bought things for her, was that it? Because most of the time she tried to compete with him. No, she didn't compete, she tried to become just like him. She shook her head. It was all too confusing. She couldn't sort it out right now.

"I guess I ought to look at the reports, since you went to so much trouble to bring them up here," she said, rising and gathering up their trays to carry back to the kitchen. "Did you say you left them on the table inside?" She left Todd to sun himself and went inside to find the financial reports.

Todd seemed to be dozing when she returned, and she leaned back in the lounge chair, studying the columns. When she saw the totals, she whistled under her breath. "Have you looked at these figures?" she asked when he sat upright, a quizzical expression on his face.

"No, George hurried me out the door before I had a chance to see them. I meant to look at them after I got here last night, but somehow I got distracted."

She handed the sheets to Todd without a word and waited while he looked. He, too, whistled when he saw the totals. "Great balls of fire," he said. "Just goes to show what can happen with the right motivation. I guess you're going to have to take full credit for this, Roxie. The contest was your idea."

A bleak expression stole across her face. "This certainly complicates things," she said, frowning. "Now I see why Daddy was so upset with me."

"What do you mean?" Todd asked.

"Didn't he say anything to you about the fight we had?" When Todd shook his head, Roxie explained how she'd wanted to call off the contest. "I decided the whole thing was misguided and I wanted to cancel. Daddy said he'd try to think of something, but he was pretty disgusted with me. Now I understand why."

"What are you going to do?" Todd asked, with a fleeting apprehension because of his own stake in the outcome. He had doubled his division's profits in his not-yet-successful fight to overtake the lead of Julian and Rusty. All that effort would be for nothing if the contest were cancelled.

"I don't know," she said, absentmindedly massaging the furrows between her eyes. "But I don't want to have to marry Julian or Rusty just because he wins the contest."

"What if neither of them wins?" Todd asked in a tight voice.

Roxie studied the financial reports and saw the gap between Todd's totals and theirs. "I don't guess there's any doubt that one or the other of them will be the winner."

"The contest isn't over yet." Todd recalled his hectic trip to Houston and the deal he'd set up too late to get on this month's report. It was so profitable that it should assure him the win. "Just suppose for a minute," he said insistently. "What would you do if you knew I'd win?"

Roxie felt a sudden chill. Marry Todd . . . because he'd won the contest? Marry Todd because it was a business arrangement? Her heart sank. "I don't know," she muttered. "How would you feel if I backed out?"

Why was she waffling and hedging like this? Surely it was clear to her by now that he'd make her a far better husband than the other VP's. Not only would he be a better business partner, but he could keep her as radiant as she was this morning. The sexual chemistry between them was dynamite. If she called off the contest . . . He felt a stabbing sense of loss at the thought. "Cheated," he said curtly. "I've worked like hell for months to win this contest. I think I'd be entitled to the reward I was promised."

"Do you really mean that?" she asked, dismayed.

"You'd insist on getting the prize even if the bride was reluctant?"

Reluctant? She didn't want him? Todd braced his body with one hand while a wave of despair washed over him. "I didn't notice any reluctance last night," he said bitterly. "I'm sure you'd get used to the idea."

"But, Todd," she protested, "don't you think the whole idea was a mistake? Don't you think people ought to marry for love, not because it's good for business?"

So she wants to wait until she falls in love, Todd thought. What she has with me isn't good enough for her. He got up from the chair and paced the deck, turning his back to hide his sinking heart. "I married once for love—or what passed for love—and it was the biggest mistake of my life. Pardon me if I don't share your romantic notions."

Roxie put on her sunglasses. She'd just as soon Todd not be able to read the stricken expression in her eyes. "Maybe you're right," she said lightly. "That's what I told Daddy when this whole thing started, that I'd never been in love in my life and probably never would be. I knew I'd never get married unless it was good for business. After all, the company is all I really care about."

"Then why did you try to back out?" Todd asked, leaning against the wooden rail of the deck. Something wasn't making sense, and she was contradicting herself with every breath.

"I guess because I'd been sick and couldn't think straight. And frankly, for a while there I got afraid that Julian or Rusty might bore me to death. But I guess that shouldn't be a problem. After all, we'll have the company in common. It'll be exciting to see how high we can run up the profits." Though the words fell brightly from Roxie's lips, she felt suddenly old and tired. "I'm glad we talked about this," she added, feeling grim. "Daddy said he thought I might change my mind after I had time to think it over. It helped a lot to hear your reaction. After all, if you'd feel cheated that Daddy called off the contest, Julian and Rusty are bound to feel the same way. It wouldn't be fair for me to renege on my obligations. It might hurt business."

Todd couldn't understand why he felt a knot in his stomach, but he was definitely nauseated. Roxie had agreed with everything he said, yet every word that fell from her lips sounded absolutely ridiculous. He must need sleep pretty badly for his head to be spinning like this. "I think I'm ready for that afternoon nap," he said. "I'm worn out." He paused, hoping against hope that she would follow him as he left the deck to go inside.

"You go ahead," she said, waving him on.

"I thought you'd made some plans for us."

"That was before we had this little talk and cleared the air. Now that my thinking is straightened out, I realize I really can't have an affair with you, Todd. After all, we'll all be working for Sunshine Enterprises, and it just wouldn't work for me to marry one of the VP's and have an affair with another."

"You aren't married yet," he said, turning toward her.

She kept her gaze on the distant shoreline. "It

would be foolish to continue something that will only cause problems later on."

"How loyal of you," Todd sneered.

"I am loyal . . . to Daddy's company."

"So I notice. Your future husband, whoever the poor jerk might be, will never have to worry about your leaving him for another man. But he damn sure might have to worry about your leaving him for a bigger company. You were born with a calculator where other people have a heart."

"Todd, please," she protested. "Let's don't fight again."

"I don't intend to fight with you, Roxie. I'm leaving."

"Perhaps that's best," she said, her body rigid in the chair.

Todd went inside to yank off his borrowed swimsuit and retrieve his own clothes from the heap where he'd left them the night before. Moments later Roxie heard a car door slam and turned her head in time to see him back out the driveway and roar back to Dallas. She took a deep breath, but she didn't cry. She'd run out of tears.

Todd burned up the highway between Denison and Dallas, driving his red 1965 Mustang convertible as though it were being pursued by the Furies. When a careless Saturday shopper pulled onto the entrance ramp at North Park directly into his path, he waved his fist and shouted curses like someone deranged. He exited on Lover's Lane and headed east through the maze of apartment complexes until he reached his own building, indistinguishable from the hundreds of others. Its anonymity had seemed desirable when he'd crawled there to lick his wounds following his divorce. Someone had swiped his parking place, so he cursed again and parked his Mustang directly behind the offending vehicle, effectively blocking it. "I'll give you a good piece of my mind when you start honking to get out," he said, with spiteful satisfaction.

He went across the sidewalk and fitted his key in the latch, immediately realizing that the door was unlocked. Puzzled, sure he'd locked it when he left, he wondered whether his apartment had been burglarized during his absence. He gingerly turned the handle and pushed open the door, stepping inside quietly in case he should surprise thieves in the act. He moved without a sound across the carpeted floor, then saw something move at the corner of his eye. He whirled, instinctively forming a fist, until he recognized the figure of his ex-wife.

"Jocelyn," he shouted. "How did you get in here?"

"I bribed your building manager," she said, her voice silky as she came toward him, her body swaying in a black dress that emphasized her long platinum hair and ivory skin. "It's good to see you, Todd," she murmured, sliding her body against his and offering her lips for his kiss.

He pushed her away and stalked to the sofa. "You've got a lot of nerve barging in here."

She followed him to the sofa and sat down, leaving a slight space between them but one which she could quickly bridge, as soon as he settled down. "I came to tell you I made a big mistake, Todd, and I want you to take me back."

He snorted. "Sure you do. What happened, did your boyfriend dump you for someone who was even more exciting? Did he get bored with your tricks so soon, Jocelyn? What a pity."

She leaned toward him, her voice purring. "I don't blame you for being angry with me, Todd. I was awful to you." Her fingers slipped out to stroke his forearm. "He was a beast, but I didn't have sense enough to realize that until it was too late." Her green eyes brimmed with tears, and she let one of them artfully slip down her cheek. "You're the one I really love, Todd. I didn't appreciate what we had until I lost it all. I was so stupid." She allowed her voice to tremble with penitence as she whispered, "Please, darling, say you'll forgive me and take me back. I'll spend the rest of my life making it up to you. I'll do anything . . . anything."

She was so close that Todd felt as though he were suffocating. He got up and paced around the small living room, realizing all at once how dowdy it was. Had his pride slipped so far that he'd lived like this for months? He'd moved into this furnished apartment without really looking at it. Night after night he'd seen nothing except a vision of Jocelyn coming back and begging his forgiveness, and now his dream had come true. She was here at the top of her form, putting on the best performance he'd ever seen. If he didn't know her so well, he might be convinced that she was really conscience-stricken.

With a growl he plopped himself on an olive green tweed chair across from her. She was just as lovely as ever. He'd always been fascinated by the paradox of her cool blonde beauty and her fiery sexual passion.

For ten years she'd used that exciting contrast to keep him eating out of her hand.

"Jocelyn, things have changed," he said at last. "I finally got over the way you walked out on me. I'll never be your puppet again, jerking and dangling when you pull the strings."

She laughed throatily. "Poor, darling Todd. Was I that hard on you?" She smiled a secret smile. "But, darling, don't you understand? I've come back to you. I'll be *your* puppet this time. I'll do anything for you. All you have to do is ask." Her eyes were full of unspoken promises.

He stared at her through narrow-slitted lids. He knew he couldn't believe a word she said, but it did something for his ego to have her come back like this. Maybe those ten years of marriage meant something to her after all. He slowly expelled his breath and relaxed. He could hardly wait to hear what she would say next.

Jocelyn realized that this was going to be harder than she'd anticipated. Todd had built a lot of defenses around himself since she'd left. She'd have to worm her way past the briars and brambles before she could win him back. She'd ease off until he let down his guard. She studied him carefully, saw dark shadows under his eyes and a deep groove along his mouth that hadn't been there when she left. But he was still good-looking, golden from plenty of sun, lean and hard-muscled. He'd let his appearance go, though; his clothes were wrinkled and grubby looking. "What have you been doing with yourself today?" she asked.

He said the first thing he could think of. "Working."

"All night?" she asked.

"How long have you been here?" he retorted, evading her question.

"I got here late last night but couldn't find you, so I came back this morning and got the manager to let me in." Her eyes traveled over Todd again; he'd always been so direct and open before, but now he seemed to be trying to hide something from her. "I suppose you're still working for Sunshine Enterprises?"

He nodded.

"How's business?"

He laughed, without mirth. "Booming, as a matter of fact."

Though she was trying to be careful about her every word and gesture, Jocelyn couldn't prevent her beautifully manicured hands from clasping together at the thought of the money Todd must be making. "George Lyons must be pleased."

Todd got up and paced again, wishing there were a real window to look out instead of two panes of glass near the ceiling. The walls seemed to be closing in on him.

"You know, Todd, you really shouldn't go to the office looking like that. I believe you need a woman around to see that your clothes get pressed. You know how George always stressed a good appearance."

"The hell with what George Lyons thinks," Todd said bitterly. He looked down at his clothes, thrown on after he'd gotten in the argument with Roxie. They were definitely the worse for wear, rumpled from their night on the floor. Todd felt a short, stabbing pain in his gut, remembering the way he and Roxie had clung to each other in the water and later in the dune, oblivious of the sand as they tumbled across it. Their passion had surpassed anything he'd ever known . . . yet Roxie could dismiss it with one snap of her fingers if it might interfere with business.

Jocelyn came to stand beside Todd, her black dress swirling gracefully. "You've been working too hard, darling," she whispered, stroking the muscles in his back. "Why don't you lie down on the sofa and let me massage away the tension?" He stiffened warily, remembering all too well how one thing always seemed to lead to another where Jocelyn was concerned. "Please, darling, come lie down," she insisted. "You're hot and tired. Let me pamper you for a little while." Her arm locked around his waist and tugged as she drew him toward the sofa, and he felt her fingers start to unfasten the buttons on his shirt.

He stopped her hands with a quick shake of his head. He wasn't about to let her see the scratches Roxie had left on his back.

Jocelyn abandoned her attempt to remove his shirt, but her fingers continued their sensual wandering, stroking him through the thin cotton fabric. "I've missed you, darling," she murmured. "And I love you so much, Todd. Please, darling, can't you find it in your heart to forgive me?" Her lips moved to his neck, his hair, then began searching for his mouth.

He twisted, evading her. If only he could believe her, Jocelyn's words might salve his wounded pride. But he knew that she was lying, and he couldn't enjoy watching her squirm like this. How could anything be so important to her that she thought she had to crawl? "Why did you come back, Jocelyn?"

"I already told you, darling. I realized what a

terrible mistake I'd made. You're the only man I'll ever love. I know that now. You're so strong, so handsome." Her fingers brushed his eyebrows, his eyelashes, but he didn't seem to be responding to her. Flattery wasn't as effective as it used to be. She took a deep breath and tried to think of something honest to say to him, something he would believe. "Do you know what I missed about you the most, darling? You were always so kind and decent. Not many men are, you know. You worked hard to give me the things I wanted, and you were generous with me." She let a few tears trickle down, wetting his cheek against hers. "No wonder you despise me, when you're so noble, and I was so cruel to you." She began to sob in a well-rehearsed imitation of shame.

Todd sighed and put his arms about her, letting her weep against his chest. She was the second woman in two days to soak the front of his shirt, and somehow he knew Jocelyn's tears were not as genuine as Roxie's had been. "Don't cry, Jocelyn. The past is past. Maybe we've both learned something from our mistakes."

He couldn't see the smile that crept across her little cat-face as she caught the scent of victory. Her tears dried almost immediately, and her arms stole around his neck. "Oh, Todd, please say you'll give me another chance." She found his lips and pressed them with her own, urging him to a response that didn't come. "I just don't know what I'll do if you don't let me come back."

"Please, Jocelyn, don't do this. I forgive you, but our marriage is over. There's nothing left between us now."

"But, Todd," she insisted, taking a calculated risk. She was going to have to be honest enough to cast herself in the role of damsel in distress and hope he was still chivalrous enough to rescue her. "I've spent all the money you gave me in our divorce settlement, and Mert Jacobs left me without a dime. I don't have any place to go. What's going to become of me?"

"I suppose you could go to work and support yourself," Todd said, sarcasm creeping into his voice. "That is, if you can't find yourself another man to take care of you."

"I deserve that," she said. She'd spent the past week looking for another man, but it was hard to find one with money on short notice. That damned Mert Jacobs had packed up and left her in Oklahoma City without any warning. With all his millions, he hadn't even left her pocket money. He must've warned his friends about her, too, because she couldn't get to first base with any of the Oklahoma oil millionaires. She could absolutely kick herself for pushing Mert too far. When she'd asked for a Russian sable and a new Mercedes all in the same week, he'd told her to hit the road. Todd just had to take her in until she could get back on her feet and find someone else.

She sneaked a look at him and saw a muscle twitching in his jaw. She hadn't expected him to be so stubborn. What could she do to break down his resistance? Seized with a sudden inspiration, she invented a preposterous lie. "Todd," she whispered, running her finger across his lips. "I didn't want to have to tell you, darling, but I guess I'll have to. I'm going to have Mert's baby, and there have been some complications. The doctor said I've got to rest until after the baby is born."

Todd sat up and stared at her in amazement. It had to be a lie. She'd never let herself get pregnant and take a chance on ruining that perfect figure of hers. "I don't believe you."

"It's true, darling," she insisted, determined to persuade him.

"Then it's simple. Mert Jacobs is worth ten million dollars. You can sue him for child support. You don't need me."

"No, darling, you're wrong," she said, her mind racing. "I will sue him later, but I can't do it now, don't you see? I'll have to wait until after the baby is born before they can do the necessary blood tests to prove paternity."

Todd put his hands around her face and held it to the light. She was a good liar, but not that good. Little drops of sweat trembled on her upper lip, and her pupils were contracted. "You're lying," he said coldly. "But I don't understand why."

Jocelyn clung to Todd, sobbing in earnest now. There was nothing else to do but tell him the truth. "Because I'm desperate," she cried. "Can't you see that? I've never worked in my life. I don't know how to take care of myself. I can't function without a man—and right now, I don't have a man. I'm broke and in two weeks I'll be on the street. What's going to become of me? I can't bear to live alone. I'd rather be dead. Please let me come back, Todd. I'll do anything if you'll just let me stay with you until I can get something worked out."

Todd felt desolate. He ached with grief to see the once-proud Jocelyn begging for crumbs. He'd thought that he wanted to see her humbled at his feet, but now that it had happened, it was an ugly sight. He didn't love her any more, but ten years of marriage had left its mark, and he felt some kind of obligation to help her if he could. He dug in his pocket and found a handkerchief, then wiped away her tears. "For God's sake, quit crying, Jocelyn. We'll work out something."

She huddled in his arms, her body shaking. "Will you let me come back?" she asked in a plaintive voice, then blew her nose on the handkerchief.

Todd raised his head and looked around the apartment. It was small, but this was an emergency. "I suppose we could put your furniture in storage," he said, trying to think. "There's not room for it here. And you won't be able to bring all your clothes because the closets are small. But I guess we can manage."

"Oh, Todd, thank you," she said, sniveling. "I knew you'd let me stay. You're too decent to do anything else." She tried to pull herself together. She'd never felt so wretched in her entire life. "I'm going to go wash my face and fix my makeup," she said, stepping out of his arms. "I hate for anybody to see me looking like this."

While she was in the bathroom, Todd walked through the apartment and tried to imagine Jocelyn living in it with him. This had been his lair while he recovered, and it violated his sense of privacy to have to share it with someone else. It was odd to realize that after sharing everything with Jocelyn for ten years, he now considered her an intruder. He was probably stupid to let her come back, but he wouldn't kick her when she was down. Maybe she'd learned her lesson and could get a new start on life. Better yet, maybe she wouldn't stay very long.

She came back into the living room gushing the most genuine thanks she was capable of.

"Jocelyn, please," he said, raising a palm to stop the flow of words. "You need help; I'm helping you. Let's just let it go at that, OK?"

She nodded. She was too exhausted to say anything else.

He reached into his vest pocket and pulled out some folded bills. "That will give you some money to operate on," he said quietly.

Jocelyn wished that he would scream at her or be stingy or something. It was horrible to have to take favors from someone who was so damned noble and generous. It made her feel cheap and tawdry. Nonetheless, she carefully counted the money and placed it in her designer leather handbag. "I'll go on back to Oklahoma City and make arrangements," she said. "Is it OK if I plan to be back here in two weeks? That's when the rent's up on my apartment there."

"Fine."

"I'm going to go on," she said, pathetically eager to make an escape. They'd run out of things to say, and Todd suddenly wondered what they would find to talk about when she came back. Everything was dead between them.

She brushed her lips against his and hurried out the door. He sank down on the sofa and put his head in his hands. The day had taken its toll, and he felt a hundred years old. At the moment he didn't care if he never saw another woman in his life. Women were nothing but trouble.

"Todd?" It was Jocelyn again, stepping back inside. "I'm sorry," she said in total disgust. "I can't leave yet. Some idiot has parked an old red convertible behind me and I can't move my car."

Without a word Todd went outside and moved the 1965 car he'd labored for months to restore to its original pristine beauty. There was no point in shaking his fist and raging at Jocelyn. She had no appreciation for classic models.

Chapter Ten

There's nothing worse than being surrounded by smiling faces when you're miserable, Roxie thought despairingly the following week as she took her seat for the August executive meeting. Julian was flying high because he'd finally managed to pull ahead of Rusty in the contest. Rusty was blissfully happy because Julian was only slightly ahead, and he had another deal on the back burner that would cook Julian's goose next month. George was glowing because Roxie had quit being difficult. She'd given him quite a scare, but bless her heart, she'd come through for him just as he'd hoped she would.

Roxie shifted in her chair to catch a glimpse of Todd. He felt her glance and lifted his head. Their eyes met for an uneasy instant before they both looked away. Roxie felt something catch in her throat and had to take a drink of water to clear it. Then she tilted her chin and forced a smile on her frozen lips.

George handled the meeting with finesse. Company profits had soared, and he gave credit where credit was due, bragging about each officer's performance but tactfully avoiding to mention that both Roxie's division and Todd's had been static during July. Everybody knew that Roxie had been ill, and Todd . . . well, Todd just needed a little more time, that's all. He was on his way back, now, after that awful divorce. His division had a wonderful month in June, so there was hope for him.

Roxie was so preoccupied with her own misery that she didn't even notice her father's unaccustomed tact. He'd never bragged about her when she did well, so she didn't think much about the fact that he didn't scold her for being off the mark in July. Todd, however, had come to the meeting fully expecting a public censure and planned to respond by listing his most recent accomplishments. He had spent most of July on the road avoiding Roxie and had finally swung a big deal with a Houston company on the last day of the month, but his profits wouldn't show up until later. But, George didn't take him to task about his poor July profits, so Todd didn't have to take the defensive. Just as well, he thought. Now he could keep his Houston deal a secret for a while longer. Maybe he could catch Julian and Rusty napping. Todd was now sure he'd win the contest. His deal was so big that nothing Julian or Rusty could dream up between now and September 30 would compare with it.

So what? he thought wearily. When he'd asked

Roxie what she'd do if she knew he would win the contest, she'd answered that she would be a reluctant bride. He'd slaved all these months to prove himself to her, and it was all for nothing. She didn't care. He turned to look more closely at Roxie. Why had everything gone sour between them? Things had been so wonderful last weekend at the lake . . . until he'd found out that she didn't want him to win the contest. His jaw clenched. Well, that's just too bad, he thought, because I'm going to win, Roxie Lyons, and I'm going to hold you to your word. You're going to marry me, no matter how reluctant you are. He glared at her across the table.

Roxie saw the contemptuous expression on Todd's face, twisting his lips so they were no longer warm and inviting. He had that mad killer look again.

"Well, fellows, that wraps things up for today. Remember, now, less than two months to go, so bust your butts!" George turned to Roxie and pinched her cheek. "Remember, the lucky man is going to win a hell of a prize."

Roxie blushed to the cheers and applause and didn't hear Todd mutter, "Hell of a prize is right."

The room emptied with the usual noisy confusion, but this time Roxie made a quick escape instead of lingering to chat. She sought the privacy of her own office, relieved to let her chin droop and put a temporary end to the phony smile she'd been forced to wear.

"Oh," she said, surprised to find Lorraine still at her desk. "Why are you working so late?"

"The phones have been so busy all week I haven't been able to get anything done," Lorraine answered.

"I wanted to get caught up while I can still read all these notes I've scribbled to myself." She closed her steno pad and tossed it in the drawer. "I guess I've done enough damage for one day. I'm going to call it quits. What about you?"

"That sounds like a winner. Let's get out of here." Roxie went to get her purse, flipping off lights as she went, so the office was cast into shadow. "Lorraine," she said as she returned, "would you like to stop for a bite to eat on the way home? I'm sure you don't want to go home and start cooking at this hour. Besides, you deserve a treat. You've had a long day."

"No longer than yours," Lorraine protested. "But, yes, I'd enjoy the chance to visit. We haven't had time to talk for a while."

"You don't have anything planned for tonight?"

"Just a quiet evening curled up with a summer rerun on television," Lorraine answered.

"Just a minute, then, and let me call the Mansion and see if they'll find a table for us."

"The Mansion? Oh, heavens, Roxie, that's too fancy!"

"You deserve a treat, remember. Besides, it's practically on the way home."

Roxie pulled her Porsche off Turtle Creek, followed by Lorraine's old brown Ford, and handed the keys to the parking attendant. The doorman ushered the two women inside the elegant entryway of the restaurant, past a huge bouquet of fresh flowers to a quiet corner table, though Roxie stopped along the way to say hello to friends.

"I'm afraid I'm not dressed for the occasion," Lorraine commented.

"Fiddlesticks. Don't you know you can go anywhere in a shirtwaist dress—as long as it's real cotton and not polyester? You look better than I do in this little sundress, but it's summertime in Dallas. What do we care what anybody thinks?"

Lorraine smiled at Roxie's self-assurance. That's the difference between the rich and the rest of us, she thought. The rich make their own rules and don't care what anybody else thinks. The rest of us spend our lives trying to conform to rules made by others. She decided to loosen up and enjoy the evening.

They ordered a cold cream of avocado soup for their appetizer, and it arrived velvety smooth, garnished with crabmeat and caviar. Roxie ate only half of hers, saving calories for the main course. They enjoyed a lively conversation, never at a loss for a topic that interested both of them, and Roxie thought how nice it was to have Lorraine for a friend. She needed someone to confide in who wouldn't condemn her.

"Are things any better between you and Todd?" Lorraine asked after the waiter had served their entree of Norwegian salmon in basil sauce with tiny julienne vegetables. "I gave him your note last week while you were up at the lake."

"He accepted my apology," Roxie answered, "but then we got into a dispute over something else. It seems that Mr. Kendrick and I don't see eye to eye on anything."

"Oh, dear. What is it this time?" Lorraine asked.

"I told him I'd asked Daddy to call off the contest so I wouldn't have to marry the winner. But Todd said I'd given my word and it would be cheating to back out."

Lorraine studied the dark shadows under Roxie's eyes, the tremor in her lower lip. "What are you going to do?" she asked, her voice soft and concerned.

"I don't know," Roxie replied, wiping her mouth with a starched white napkin. "If I back out, everybody will be mad at me. But if I stay in, I'll have to marry somebody I don't love just because he won the stupid contest." She took a sip of wine and felt her eyes fill with tears. "I tried to tell Daddy how I felt, and he said he'd help me worm out of it if that's what I really wanted. But, Lorraine, I could tell he was disappointed in me. I've never let him down before, and I just don't know if I can do it now. Especially not when it means Todd and everybody else will be mad at me, too."

Lorraine placed her fork on her empty plate so the waiter could clear the table and bring dessert. For a moment she pondered Roxie's statement and realized that Roxie wasn't at all the blithe spirit she appeared to be. While she might shrug off some of the conventions, she was really a slave to the whims of others because she needed their approval so much. Roxie might not have any qualms about wearing a cotton sundress to a fancy restaurant, but she couldn't bear to disappoint her father. "Why did you change your mind about the contest, Roxie?" she asked. "I thought you said earlier that you were never going to fall in love, anyway."

"I didn't think I would—after all, I never had, and it seemed like it would already have happened if it was ever going to." She lifted her eyes to Lorraine's and found only sympathetic understanding. "But I didn't know I was going to fall in love with Todd Kendrick."

Lorraine reached out to press Roxie's hand. "I wondered if that wasn't what happened," she said, sighing. "That certainly makes it difficult, doesn't it?" She wrinkled her brow in thought, then said, more cheerfully, "Maybe Todd will win the contest. It's not over yet."

"But, Lorraine, don't you see?" Roxie wailed. "I don't want Todd to marry me because of the *contest.* I love him, and I don't want him to marry me unless he loves me, too."

"I see your point," Lorraine said, patting Roxie's hand. The waiter interrupted their conversation to serve dessert, a beautiful fruit tart with kiwi, melon and banana. "Umm, this is perfect for a hot summer evening."

"I'm not going to eat the crust," Roxie said. "I bet it's loaded with butter." She speared a bite of the green kiwi with its inner ring of edible black seeds and swallowed the mellow, tangy fruit. "It's delicious," she said. "Too bad I've lost my appetite. What's wrong with you when you can't eat or sleep or concentrate?"

"I think they call that lovesickness," Lorraine said with a gentle smile.

Roxie traced ovals on the white tablecloth with her spoon. "I must have a good case of it, then. I can't seem to think about anything except . . ." A light pink flush crept up Roxie's neck as she remembered the way Todd's arms had felt, holding her close while he made love to her.

"Usually lovesickness is a very contagious disease," Lorraine said, noting the brilliance in Roxie's eyes. "Couples tend to catch it from each other the same way they do mono. Don't you suppose Todd is running a slight fever of his own?"

"No, I don't think so," Roxie said glumly. "He says he's only interested in my father's money. At first I didn't believe it, but now I know it's true. That's why he got so mad when I told him I wanted to call off the contest."

"Oh, dear." Lorraine sipped her coffee and tried to think of a way to help her beloved Roxie, but it seemed hopeless. She looked so depressed that Lorraine tried to distract her with casual conversation about the Dallas heat wave and new fall fashions, and they finished their dinner without further mention of Todd or the contest. Roxie paid the check, then waited with Lorraine while the valet brought their cars around, before going home to spend another restless night.

She woke in the middle of the night crying over a dream she'd had. She sat up in bed, trying to remember the bits and pieces of the dream and feeling an aching sadness. She'd been haunted often lately with nightmares of herself as a child at her dance recital, and in this dream the audience was composed of all the men in her life. Her father was in the front row with Todd beside him, and Julian and Rusty were there, too. She danced and danced, doing first a slow soft shoe. When nobody clapped, the tempo quickened and she did a feisty tap dance, but still there was no applause. She did the Cotton Eyed Joe followed by a jazz ballet, but nothing was good enough to merit their applause. The men began to grow in size, and she felt herself shrinking on the stage, surrounded by the huge angry faces that loomed over her. The music became increasingly difficult, and she tried desperately to find an appropriate dance for each selection, performing solitary waltzes and schottisches and polkas until she collapsed, exhausted and shriveled to the size of a rag doll. The music stopped, and the house lights came up. The audience rose with furious shouts and left the auditorium, silent and empty now except for Roxie, huddled and weeping alone onstage.

"I can't go on this way," Roxie sobbed into her pillow. "I've done the best I can, but it's never what they want from me. I'm through trying to do the impossible. Damn it, Daddy, from now on I'm going to please myself!"

It was with some apprehension that Roxie went into her father's office the following morning and shut the door. Both high-tempered, they'd had many fierce arguments over the years, but never before had Roxie defied her father and done something which he adamantly opposed. She wasn't sure that she could do it now, but she had to try. Her whole personality was at stake.

George was all smiles as she entered the room, because he was still caught up in the good will of yesterday's executive meeting and the company's soaring profits. "Come in, princess," he boomed. "Have you seen the *Wall Street Journal* this morning?

There's an article about hot real estate projects, and Sunshine Enterprises got a very favorable mention."

"That's wonderful, Daddy," Roxie replied, trying to muster some enthusiasm. "I'm sure the price of our stock will go even higher."

"You bet it will," George said, tilting back in his big leather chair. "Why, that 5 percent of outstanding stock the winner of the contest is going to get may be worth a million and a half instead of a piddling million."

"Daddy, I want to talk to you about that," Roxie said, squaring her shoulders.

"Now, sweetheart, you know I don't mind a bit giving away a hunk of change like that. After all, there's nothing better to spend it on than making my baby girl happy."

"Daddy, please." She sat down on a chair across from him and leaned across the desk, her face intent. "We've got to talk about the contest. I can't go through with it."

George lowered his chair with a thud. "We talked about it last week, Roxie. Remember, I explained to you that it's too late to call things off now?"

"I remember you told me you'd call it off if I really wanted you to."

They frowned at each other across the desk. "Roxie, you're still tired, sweetheart," George said, trying to contain his rising irritation. "I think you need a few more days at the lake."

"What are you going to do, keep me up there for six more weeks until the contest is over?"

"If that's what it takes to bring you to your senses." George got up and came around the desk to put his arm around Roxie. "You've been working too hard and it's scrambled your brain. You need some rest, sweetheart."

She turned her ashen face toward him and clenched her fists. "Daddy, please listen to me. I know you're disappointed in me. I know you think I've let you down. But no matter how much it hurts you, I simply cannot go through with this contest. Won't you try to understand that?"

George rammed his fists in his pockets and stalked over to the corner of the room. "I don't see how you expect me to call it off at this late date. It's gone too far, Roxie."

"Don't say that, Daddy. I'm your daughter, not some real estate project. This is my life we're talking about." She got up and started toward him, wanting more than anything for him to hold her close and say he understood. "Daddy, please." She tried to put her arms around him, but he stepped out of reach.

"Is this your final word on this?" he asked. He was as distraught as Roxie, and his voice was trembling with anger and disapproval. "No matter how disappointed I am, you won't change your mind?"

She stood rock-still, her arms rigid at her sides. She'd hoped that he'd understand, but Daddy was never going to change. He was too old and too set in his ways. Building a business empire was the most important thing in his life, and his daughter was only a pretty bauble to decorate his business achievements. He loved her, but only on his own terms.

She lifted her head and studied him as though she were seeing him for the first time. His face was flushed, as it always was when he was angry, making his white hair look even whiter. His skin was wrinkled, with brown age spots on his cheeks and forehead. His ears and nose seemed larger now than they'd been when she was a child, and his eyebrows seemed more bristly. But he still towered over her, bigger than life itself, and no matter how furious he made her, she loved him. He was her father, her hero, the man who'd spoiled and pampered her all her life. Her breath caught tremulously as she remembered how proud of him she'd been when she was a little girl. Her father was the most handsome, most wonderful daddy of all, and her greatest joy had been having him scoop her into his arms with a big hug and parade her in front of the whole world. Oh, what a twosome they were, strutting and smiling together!

How could she bear to let go of all that, to give up the sunshine of Daddy's approval? She felt a chill and shuddered involuntarily. Things would never be the same again. Her father would still love her, but he would have reservations. It wouldn't be the sweeping, unrestrained love he gave her now.

She reached out to touch his face. He was really getting old. Somehow she hadn't noticed that before. Was it wrong to hurt him this way, when his time was growing short? Maybe she should let things rock along in the same old way. She was still young and strong, and besides that, she was a survivor. She could get through this no matter what happened. Maybe she should . . . She felt his leathery skin under her fingers and wondered what life would be like without him. She was gripped with a sense of loss.

And yet to win her father's approval would require her to smother her self. She had finally come face to face with her blundering values and realized that people were more important than business, the heart more enduring than profits. Could she deny these truths in order to appease him and earn his indulgent praise? Sadly she shook her head.

"Daddy, I'm sorry."

George closed his big paw over Roxie's hand and lifted it to his lips. "Oh, hell, princess, you do what you have to do."

"You'll forgive me?"

"You don't give me much choice, do you? I couldn't make it without my baby girl." He hugged her against him, and Roxie realized that his muscles were flabby, his chest sunken. He was an old man, no longer a proud warrior parading before her. Tears sprang to her eyes.

"I love you, Daddy."

"I love you, too, princess."

"I wish it didn't have to be this way."

He sighed. "Oh, well. I've brought this company through two wars and seven recessions. I'll get through this little personnel problem, too."

"I'll help you."

"If you don't mind, Roxie, I think I'd just as soon handle it without you. You've helped me a little too much already."

She pulled back her head to see his face and found that he was smiling through a mist of tears. She threw her arms around his neck and hugged him, her own tears wetting his neck. "Oh, Daddy, thank you."

"For what?"

"For being my daddy," she answered simply, kissing his lined cheek.

He rumpled her hair and squeezed her. "I think you better run along," he said in a choked voice. "It looks like I'm going to have a busy day."

Lorraine barely had time to note the glassy expression on Roxie's face before she was summoned into George's office. He dictated a few letters in a preoccupied way and grumbled about the latest batch of invoices for office supplies. "Damn it, Lorraine, tell those secretaries to quit wasting stuff. How many rolls of correction tape does it take to run this company, anyway?"

"I bought a six-month supply," Lorraine answered. "It's cheaper in quantity."

"Oh." He bent forward in his chair and propped his head on his elbows. "Sorry to be so irritable this morning. Roxie just dealt me a bad hand of cards, and I'm trying to figure out what to do about it."

"Is it something about the contest?" she asked.

"Yep. Did she say something to you about it?"

"A little. We had dinner together last night, and I knew she was upset."

"I don't know what's come over her, Lorraine. She's always been such a good girl, never giving me a minute's trouble. Now all at once she's so moody and unpredictable I never know what to expect from her. Would you believe she actually wants me to call off the contest?"

"Will you?"

George buried his head in his hands. "I don't know. I told her I would . . . but if I do that, the whole thing will lose momentum and come to a screeching halt, with six weeks left to go. Hell, I don't see why I have to tell the fellows now and cut the contest short. Maybe she'll change her mind again."

"I don't know," Lorraine said skeptically. "It sounded to me like her mind was made up."

"What do you think I ought to do?" George leaned back and peered at Lorraine. She'd worked for him for thirty years, and he trusted her judgment. She was solid and dependable with an abundance of common sense.

"I think you ought to keep your promise," she answered, without even pausing.

"Which promise? The one to Roxie or the one to my boys?"

She was not impressed with the way George was trying to wiggle his way out of this problem. "If you're going to look at it that way, then I guess you have to decide which is most important to you."

George howled with indignation. "Lorraine, I'm caught between a rock and a hard place, and the least you could do is give me a little sympathy."

"Sorry, I just gave all my sympathy to Roxie. You're a tough old boot, George, and you can get along just fine without it."

"So, you women are going to gang up on me, is that it?" He looked at Lorraine in absolute astonishment. "After all these years I have a mutiny right under my nose?"

"Maybe we'd all have been better off if we'd rebelled a long time ago." She snapped the cover on her shorthand book. "If that's all the dictation, I'll go type these letters."

"Now, just a minute. I'd like to know what's going on around here, anyway. Roxie's throwing tantrums and you're in a huff. Why is everybody mad at me?"

"Nobody's mad at you, George," Lorraine replied, but her lips were set in a thin line that belied her words. "Roxie just decided the contest was a bad idea, that's all."

"It turned out to be bad for my relationship with Roxie, but it's been wonderful for business. Did you see the *Wall Street Journal* today?"

"No, but I heard about it." She shook her head when George tried to hand her the newspaper. "George, can't you forget about *business* for one minute? Your daughter needs your help."

George threw up his arms in despair. "I'm trying to find a way to help her without wrecking my business."

"Can't you call an executive meeting and explain what happened? I'm sure everybody will understand."

"What? Stop the contest before it's over? I forbid you to mention such a thing."

"But, George—"

"No buts. If Roxie doesn't change her mind, I'll tell them on October 1 when I announce the winner of the contest. But not one day sooner, do you hear me?" He pounded the desk in emphasis. "I'm not going to lose the wallop the guys have built up."

"George, you will tell them on October 1, won't you? You won't hold Roxie to her promise?"

He pushed his gnarled fingers through his white hair. "I give you my word. But I want absolute secrecy until October 1."

Lorraine breathed a sigh of relief. For a minute

there George had her worried. "Who do you think is going to win?" she asked.

George shook his head. "Hard to tell. Julian pulled ahead last month, but I don't know whether he can keep his lead. Some of his investments are in Mexico, and the currency situation down there may hurt him. I think Rusty will probably squeak past him."

"You don't think Todd has a chance?"

"Doesn't look that way. He got a slow start, and that Florida project never got off the ground. He can't possibly win unless he pulls something out of a hat." George noticed a wistful expression on Lorraine's face. "Why do you ask?"

"Just wondering. I'd like to see Todd win, that's all."

"There's not much chance of that now. Besides, I think he may have to disqualify himself." He walked around the desk and poured himself a cup of coffee without observing Lorraine's frown.

"But why, George?"

"I heard a rumor at the country club last night that his ex-wife is coming back. That oil man from Oklahoma dumped her, so she came running home to Todd."

George turned when he heard Lorraine gasp. "Oh, no," she cried. "Does Roxie know?"

"I forgot to mention it to her in all the excitement this morning. I bet she'll be glad he's out of the running. She can't stand the guy."

Lorraine couldn't hold back an uneasy chuckle. "Where have you been the past month, George? Don't you realize she's in love with him? That's why she backed out of the contest."

"Roxie's in love with Todd? That's why she backed

out of the contest?" George was too surprised to say a word for several hushed minutes. "Why didn't you tell me sooner?" he asked as soon as he could speak again.

"She's *your* daughter. I thought you'd have noticed, the way they've both been acting lately."

"Both? You mean Todd's in love with Roxie, too?"

"Roxie doesn't think so." Lorraine kept her eyes on her steno pad.

"What do you think?" George stared at Lorraine until she was forced to lift her head and meet his penetrating gaze.

"I thought he had all the signs of a man in love—until you told me he took Jocelyn back. Now I don't know what to think."

George waved his arms in agitation. "Never mind that. I'm sure she isn't coming to stay. My guess is she's just using Todd for a meal ticket until she latches on to someone else." George walked to the window, hunching his head into his shoulders while he tried to think. "A meal ticket, maybe . . . or a launching pad."

"What do you mean?"

"I mean that beautiful, clever, scheming little Jocelyn probably figures she can meet more eligible men through Todd than she can on her own."

"Well, I'd hate for Jocelyn to screw things up for them."

George rocked back and forth on the balls of his feet until the glimmer of an idea formed in the back of his mind. He began to smile, then burst into whooping laughter until tears rolled down his cheeks. "Lorraine, you just quit your worrying and let nature take its course—with a little assistance from good old Dad." He reached in his pocket for a handkerchief to wipe his eyes. "Roxie and Todd and Jocelyn—a regular alleycat brawl!"

When Lorraine took her steno pad and slipped out the door, George was still laughing. Over her shoulder she could hear him guffaw, "And may the best man win."

Chapter Eleven

The rest of August passed in a busy whirl, and Roxie experienced a sense of freedom she'd never known before. After a lifetime of adjusting her behavior to please her father, she found it exhilarating to strive for self-esteem. She was learning to give herself credit for doing a good job and was thereby liberated from the compulsion to earn praise from others. No longer constrained to be "Daddy's good little girl," the pendulum took a swing in the opposite direction, and she sometimes challenged George simply to savor the heady experience. She began to stretch her wings, learning what *she* liked and wanted, and she found to her surprise that she could enjoy the company of men without flirtation games. She lowered her defenses enough to express her true feelings, at least on occasion, and found that people were just as intrigued by the "real" Roxie as they'd been by the one she'd created to entertain and cajole them.

When she learned that Todd's ex-wife had returned, she wrote him a note saying, "I hope this time things will work out for you. You deserve the best." She hurriedly gave the note to Lorraine and asked her to deliver it before she changed her mind, then spent the rest of the afternoon shredding bits of paper and tossing them into the wastebasket.

Todd read the note and started to call Roxie to say that he and Jocelyn were not attempting a reconciliation. Then he decided that it was too complicated to explain, and besides, it was none of Roxie's business. He would settle things with her when he won the contest, and in the meantime, let Roxie believe that there was someone who appreciated him. She'd bruised his ego, and he'd be damned if he'd let her find out how much.

The August profit figures were released, showing that Rusty had jumped to first place in the contest and Julian had fallen to third, leaving Todd in second. Roxie sat glumly through the September executive meeting, wishing George would break the news that she had cancelled the contest. She hated the idea of letting the competition continue for another whole month and realized that she would have to find some tangible way to make amends to the winner. George cut the meeting short with the reminder that everybody was expected at Lake Texoma for the company picnic on Labor Day. This year's picnic would be the best ever because he wanted to reward everybody for their fantastic efforts the past five months and was sparing no expense.

"Y'all bring your friends and families, now, and we're going to have a great time. Everybody take the weekend off and get rested up for the last sprint across the finish line. Remember, boys, September 30 is just around the corner, so bust your butts!"

The meeting broke up, and Roxie and Todd cast furtive glances at each other trying to decide whether or not to work their way through the crowd to exchange a few words. George caught Roxie just as she was about to maneuver herself in Todd's direction and said, "I'd like for you to go up to the lodge with me on Sunday evening and be sure everything is all set, OK?"

"Sure, if you need me." They had hired the best caterer in Dallas as well as a recreation director to bring equipment for every conceivable sport or activity, but Roxie knew everything would have to have a final inspection. An all-day picnic for several hundred employees needed careful planning.

"I've asked Lorraine to come, too. She'll be a big help, and besides, I kind of enjoy her company."

Roxie paused in her imperceptible drift toward Todd to give her father a surprised look. "I'm glad to hear that," she said, "because Lorraine has become my dearest friend."

George added several complimentary remarks about Lorraine, and by the time he'd finished, Todd had made his way to their corner. George tried to read their faces as Todd and Roxie nodded greetings, but they were too cagey to reveal themselves. Ready to launch his private scheme to get rid of Jocelyn, George turned to Todd and said, "You're planning to bring Jocelyn with you to the picnic, aren't you? I've missed that pretty little face of hers."

Todd, caught off guard, replied evasively, but George insisted with the high-handedness borne of a lifetime of tyranny to subordinates. Finally Todd had no choice but to agree, though he nearly strangled on the words. With Jocelyn complicating his life right now, Todd had intended to skip the company picnic this year, and now he was stuck just like a pig on a spit.

Roxie watched the pained expression on Todd's face and realized that George had put him in an uncomfortable position. For a moment Roxie considered poking her father in his soft belly with her fist. It would serve him right to have the wind knocked out of him. But as usual, George saved his most outrageous behavior for crowded places, where calling his hand would create a public scene. At the moment there was nothing Roxie could do except grit her teeth. She shot Todd a sympathetic glance, and he quickly made his escape before George could ask any embarrassing questions about Jocelyn.

George was suddenly wary of the gleam in Roxie's eye and took a backward step, saying, "We'll pick you up at six o'clock Sunday night. See you then." He beat a hasty retreat, chuckling under his breath. He could hardly wait for the Labor Day picnic.

Roxie was up early Labor Day morning, knowing that company employees would soon arrive from Dallas in full force. She had spent a quiet Sunday evening with George and Lorraine at the lodge, doing her best to fight down memories of the night she'd spent there with Todd. She took a quick swim with the others, but absolutely refused to take a canoe ride. She doubted that she'd ever get in a canoe again. The reminder would be too painful.

She dressed in citrus green tailored slacks and a brightly printed blouse tied to expose her bare midriff. At least she *looked* cheerful, she thought as she applied blusher and eyeliner, then scads of mascara.

George had gallantly insisted upon sleeping in the bunkroom so that Roxie and Lorraine could have the privacy of separate bedrooms. When Roxie went into the kitchen, she found George and Lorraine there ahead of her, talking quietly so they wouldn't wake her. George laughed at something Lorraine said, and Roxie realized that she hadn't heard her father laugh in a long time. It warmed her heart to hear him sound so happy.

"Good morning, sleepy head," he said as she came in to pour a cup of coffee and join them.

"Daddy, it's only seven o'clock. This is a holiday, remember?"

"The caterer has been here since six. Can you smell the charcoal? He's going to finish up the barbecued brisket and spareribs he started in town yesterday and then cook up a big breakfast for the folks who come early."

"I guess people will stuff themselves and then nobody will want to do anything but lie around all day."

"Not if history repeats itself. There'll be a softball game going by nine o'clock, and volleyball, and horseshoes—"

"And a big group will take a boat ride, maybe fish a little," Lorraine added. "The kids will swim and eat hot dogs and marshmallows all day and go home tonight with a stomach ache and a sunburn."

"Wouldn't be Labor Day without it," George said, pushing back his chair to go outside and get started. It was a beautiful day, too good to waste. "I want to talk to that caterer and be sure they brought a freezer of strawberry ice cream. Last year they forgot and we only had three kinds," he grumbled, "peach, vanilla and peppermint."

"You're having homemade ice cream for three hundred people?" Roxie asked in astonishment.

"Roxie, you can't have a decent picnic with store-bought ice cream. Besides, the kids get a kick out of cranking it and fighting over who gets to lick the paddle."

"I hope your Wall Street friends never find out the truth about Sunshine Enterprises. They think it's a sophisticated Dallas corporation, and here's the president licking icing off a cake with his finger."

George snatched his hand away from the foil-wrapped cake he'd been poking, and they laughed together when he colored.

A couple of hours later, two cars pulled into the driveway simultaneously, the first arrivals, and they went outside to greet their colleagues and admire their kids. Roxie held her breath. The Labor Day picnic had begun.

It was almost noon before Todd arrived with Jocelyn. He'd deliberately waited until time for lunch and had every intention of making his appearance and leaving as soon as possible. The whole situation was a nightmare, and he was glad that they didn't yet convict people for homicidal thoughts. Otherwise what he itched to do to George Lyons would get Todd a life sentence—without parole.

Things were awkward enough between Todd and Jocelyn without the additional pressure of a crowd and a command performance. Jocelyn had been living at Todd's apartment for the past two weeks, taking over his bedroom while he'd moved to the sofa in the living room. She was still sleeping when he left each morning, and he stayed at work until late in the day to avoid going home. Sometimes she would be out with friends when he returned, sometimes she'd already gone to bed. But sometimes she was awake, and they had to make stilted conversation.

Jocelyn had made little progress in finding a new male companion, and she was overjoyed when Todd invited her to attend the company picnic with him. There would be a number of eligible men present, and she was ready to attach herself to anybody to escape currying favor with Todd. Maybe she could find someone who was more her type and who would appreciate her. Besides, she was getting lonely in that big empty bed.

Todd had to park his red Mustang down the road a quarter mile from the lodge because there were so many cars ahead of him. Jocelyn bounced out on the passenger side, eager to join the party, and had to keep stopping to wait for Todd to catch up with her. He stumped along, head down, until they reached the grassy slope where picnic tables had been set up and a noisy crowd had assembled. He paused, took his sunglasses from the pocket of his mahogany brown knit shirt and put them on to screen his eyes, not from the sun but from inquisitive glances. He checked to be sure his shirttail was neatly tucked into his chino slacks, straightened his collar and smoothed his hair. Then, forcing a smile, he placed his hand at the small of Jocelyn's back and moved forward.

George had not allowed himself to become too busy to watch for Todd and Jocelyn, and had seen them long before they reached the lodge. He hurried forward with genuine warmth and acute curiosity, a puckish grin on his face. "There you are, son, glad you could make it," he said, clapping Todd on the back. He turned to Jocelyn with a hearty handshake but, contrary to Todd's expectations, asked no awkward questions.

George made a few remarks about the contest and how it had stimulated business, alluding to the million dollars' worth of stock which the winner would receive but carefully failing to mention that the grand prize was Roxie's hand in marriage. Jocelyn pricked up her ears at the mention of money and asked in a feathery voice who the front runners were, taking note that the answer was now Rusty and Julian. His objective accomplished, George put his arm around Jocelyn and said he'd show her around himself and see that she was amused. "You leave this pretty little lady to me, son, and you go down there to the barbecue pits and have Roxie fix you a big plate of spareribs before they're all gone. You've been looking a little thin lately, so you eat hearty and get some meat back on those bones."

He gave Todd a slight push and hesitated just long enough to be sure he headed in Roxie's direction, then steered Jocelyn over to join Rusty and Julian at their table. "Let me find you something decent to drink, honey. I'll bring you some of my good Scotch from the lodge. You stay right here and let these two look after you until I get back." By the time George got back with the Scotch, Jocelyn had one hand on Rusty's shoulder and the other on Julian's knee and didn't even notice that George had left the drink and disappeared.

Roxie turned when she heard footsteps behind her and automatically picked up a plate before she realized that it was Todd approaching the food-laden table. "Oh," she said, "hello, Todd. It's good to see you." Her eyes met his in a shy glance, both of them suddenly aware of the last time they'd been at the lodge together.

Todd's eyes traveled from her thick, glossy hair to her sandaled feet, appreciating every stop in between. "How do you manage to look so beautiful all the time?" he asked, reaching out to brush a tendril of hair away from her cheek.

His touch raised little goosebumps on Roxie's skin, and she lifted her hand and placed it against his. "If that's a compliment, thank you very much."

A child jostled against them. "Where's some more lemonade?" he asked insistently. "I'm thirsty."

"At the other end of the table in that big red container. See it?" Roxie sent the boy on his way and turned to Todd. "Let me fix you a plate. Everybody says the spareribs are wonderful."

"Haven't you tried them for yourself?"

"Not yet. I've been too busy fixing plates for everybody else."

Todd looked around at the crowd of people, all eating and talking in small groups spread over the yard and decks. "Everybody seems to be doing OK. Why don't you fix two plates and let's see if we can find a quiet place to sample the barbecue?"

"I don't know whether I can leave. They'll all be wanting ice cream any minute."

Todd picked up a plate and handed it to Roxie. "I'll take one of everything," he said. "All at once I'm starving." He started toward the lodge but paused when Roxie called his name.

"Where are you going?" she asked.

"To get George. The ice cream was his idea. He'll be glad to dish it up while you take a break." Todd raced up the grassy slope and found George arm-wrestling with a freckle-faced ten-year-old. Only too glad to be rescued from certain defeat, George followed Todd back to the picnic table and cast a critical eye over the plates Roxie had filled during Todd's absence.

"Better put another rib or two on Todd's plate," he cautioned. "And get him an extra sourdough biscuit. He's been looking a little peaked lately." George made additions to the plate until it was heaped high, despite Todd's protests that he'd never be able to eat so much food. "You two run along and enjoy your meal. I'll keep an eye on things here." George smiled to himself as Roxie and Todd worked their way through the crowd and headed toward the beach. Even if it was Labor Day and half the people in Texas had come to Lake Texoma, George would bet a thousand dollars that those two would find themselves a private spot. . . .

They went far enough down the beach to be out of sight of the Sunshine employees, though it was impossible to find total seclusion on a crowded holiday. They found a high dune formed by the tides that protected them from prying eyes on three sides but was easily visible to passengers on the numerous boats in the area. Todd dropped to the sand, balancing his plate, then offered his hand to Roxie while she lowered herself beside him. The sand filled her sandals, so she kicked them off, enjoying the squish as she burrowed her bare toes. Todd propped his plate on his bent knees and leaned against the back of the dune, needing both hands to eat the messy, but delicious, spareribs.

While they ate, they talked, carefully avoiding the subjects that had led to past arguments. It had been a long, hard month for both of them since they'd made love and quarreled, and they were so glad to be together again that they were determined not to let anything spoil it for them. By the time they finished eating they were a mess, with barbecue sauce on their hands and faces as well as butter from the corn on the cob. They'd forgotten to bring paper napkins, so they walked a few feet to the lake and dipped their hands and splashed their faces, then dried themselves as well as they could with Todd's clean handkerchief. The sun beat down with a noontime intensity, so they were quick to return to the shade of the dune.

Todd stretched out alongside the marsh grass and patted the sand, beckoning Roxie to join him. She dropped to her feet in one graceful motion and sat, leaning against him with one hand propped on his shoulder.

"I've missed you," he murmured in a husky voice, putting an arm around her waist to draw her closer.

"Have you? I heard you had . . . other company these days."

"If you mean Jocelyn, yes, she's back—for the time being."

Roxie averted her head. "I hope you'll be able to work things out."

"Fat chance," he answered with a cynical laugh. "She'll be gone again as soon as she finds some new man to bankroll her."

"And you don't mind?" Roxie asked in surprise.

Todd gave a disgusted grunt. "After the hell she's put me through? Once I was so stupid I thought I couldn't live without her, but now I'm a sadder but wiser man. I wouldn't have her back on a bet."

"Oh . . . I thought—"

"Don't think," he said firmly. "It's over. For good."

The heaviness that had filled Roxie's heart for the past two weeks disappeared like a vapor, and in its place was a sudden giddiness. Contrary to her fears, Todd was free after all. Even if he didn't love her in return, at least he wasn't bound to someone else. She felt an overwhelming urge to laugh.

She used her free hand to trace old laugh lines at the corner of his eyes and mouth, the newer furrows in his forehead. This was the first time she'd been close to Todd since she'd realized she was in love with him, and she studied him now as though she would memorize every pore in his skin, every fleck of gold in his brown eyes. There was a tiny scar near one eye she'd never noticed, a small ridge of bone in his nose that kept it from being perfectly straight. A summer in the sun had bleached his hair, so that it was darker at the base of his head and golden on the ends. It was thick and silky to her touch, and in the summer heat it curled along his neckline and sideburns. Her fingertips stroked his cheekbones, traced his jawline and chin, then brushed against his throat to the open neck of his brown shirt, where curly golden hairs tickled her fingers. Her hands moved across the hard ridge of his collarbone, and she could feel the strength of his shoulder muscles under the knit fabric.

Todd lay perfectly still under the detailed examination performed by her fingers, looking up into her sparkling blue eyes almost without breathing. The noise of the picnic sounded far away, and here in the dune they could hear only the soft lapping of the waves against the sand. Roxie lifted her hand and traced the outline of Todd's lips with her long fingernail, then smiled at him. She'd never seen a more handsome man in her life, not even in the movies.

"Hey," he said, reaching to still her hand. "You've got to stop looking at me like that."

"Like what?" She leaned down and brushed his nose with her own, Eskimo-style.

"I don't know exactly . . . like you might never see me again, maybe." His hand moved to her back and pulled her down beside him on the sand. "Whatever it is, it's scary."

He folded her in the crook of his arm, his chest against her back, and rested his chin against her ear. His hand reached out to trace the clothed outline of her waist, the curve of her hip, the smooth expanse of her thigh. She could feel the hammer of his heart against her shoulder blade, the fabric of his trousers against her bare foot. It was heavenly to lie in his arms like this, safe and cherished, at least for now. She couldn't let the moment slip away.

"Todd," she whispered, turning in his arms to face him.

"Oh, God, Roxie, I told you to stop looking at me like that." His powerful arms closed around her, pulling her so close she couldn't breathe and didn't care.

"Todd," she said before he could bend his head to kiss her. "Look at me and tell me what it is that frightens you."

"I told you. It's like maybe you were never going to see me again."

"No, that isn't what it is."

"But it's like you're trying to memorize every single thing about me."

"Yes . . . yes, I am."

"But why?"

"Can't you tell?"

Todd lifted himself on one elbow and gazed down at Roxie. Her eyes met his without flinching, open to his scrutiny in a way she'd never permitted before. She lowered all her defenses and left herself completely vulnerable to him, holding back nothing. Her love was there for him to see . . . if he dared. She held her breath while a heavy, brooding silence filled the private world of their sand dune.

He peered into her eyes and was startled at the tenderness he saw there. He quickly moved his glance to her lips and found a warm, poignant smile. What had happened to the brittleness, the mischief, the flirtation that had been her suit of armor? He thought back to that night so long ago when he'd told her he wanted to know her as a real person . . . but he'd never dreamed it would be so terrifying when she let down her barricades and exposed herself to him. A choking sensation constricted his throat. He didn't know how to react to the discovery that she was neither tough nor feisty, but was instead—

"Roxie," he whispered, running his finger down her cheek. "You scare me to death."

"Why?"

"Because I'm used to that prickly exterior of yours. I don't recognize you when you're like this."

"You used to give me a hard time because I wouldn't let you know me as a real person."

"Yeah. Strange, isn't it?"

"No, not really," she answered, shifting a little to watch the play of light and shadow in the marsh grass. "I guess it's just as frightening to know another person as it is to let someone know you. We've traded places, that's all."

"You're not afraid any more?"

She shook her head in response.

"Why not?"

"I guess because I finally stopped running from the truth."

She was talking in riddles. "What truth?" he asked, a little impatiently.

"I think you have to discover that for yourself," she said softly, lifting her eyes to his.

Her dewy expression made his stomach turn somersaults, and he caught his breath. He framed her face with his big hands and studied the glowing embers that lit her eyes, turning them a deep, sapphire blue. Her pupils were huge with emotion, and he could sense, rather than see, a mist of tears. Her whole heart was in her eyes at that moment.

"Roxie, it's not . . ."

"I love you, Todd."

"But you can't," he objected. "When did it—"

Roxie shrugged. "I don't know. It just snuck up on me." She waited to see what he'd say next and almost wished she hadn't revealed herself. It was frightening to make a declaration of love to someone who didn't love in return. She'd hoped he'd be pleased, or touched, or at least flattered, but he sat motionless in the sand, too stunned to say anything at all. She began to toy nervously with the stems of marsh grass that lined the dune. So much for honesty and being your own true self, she thought despairingly.

"Hey," he whispered, "don't be unhappy, Roxie." She felt his arms fold around her, and he lifted her from the sand and cuddled her against his chest. "I'm surprised, that's all. I stopped believing in love months ago, and I thought you had, too."

She sighed heavily against his chest. "That was before we—"

He chuckled against her hair. "Are you sure you're not confusing love with old-fashioned lust?"

"Todd, don't make fun of me," she protested. "This is the first time in my whole life I've ever told a man I loved him, and the least you can do is take me seriously. I'm sure this is an experience I'm never going to repeat." She sat up in his arms and dusted the sand from her clothes. "Please don't take all the joy out of it for me."

Despite her frustration, Roxie felt the inner glow that comes with giving voice to love, and her face was radiant. Her beauty took on a new translucence that gave Todd pause, and in his most obliging manner he said, "I beg your pardon. Let's start all over, shall we?"

"Excellent suggestion," she answered. "Now, where were we? . . . Oh, yes." She turned to face Todd and placed her hands on his shoulders. "Todd, I have something very important to say to you."

He tilted her chin and gazed with real affection into her eyes. "Please tell me at once," he said. "I'm anxious to hear what it is."

"I love you, my darling." A triumphant smile lit her face. "Oh, Todd, I do love you so." She flung herself into his arms and lifted her face. "Please kiss me."

There was no pretense in Roxie's enthusiasm, and she kissed him as wholeheartedly as she'd proclaimed her love. Her lips yielded to Todd's with a sweet urgency that invited him to plunder her mouth, tasting its moist hollows. His tongue darted out to caress hers, then sought the sensitive roof of her mouth and teased it with exciting strokes. Her breathing quickened, and he tore his mouth from hers and buried it in the tender hollow of her throat, kissing and licking the delicate skin until she moaned with pleasure.

His fingers sought the knot tied at the front of her shirt and jerked it loose, then moved instinctively to her soft breast, tearing at the bra which hindered him.

"Todd, don't," she whispered, letting her head fall backward as his mouth moved down her body. "Someone will see us."

Dazed, he lifted his eyes and scanned the nearby waters. "There aren't any boats close to shore," he said. "Keep your back to the lake. As long as you have your shirt on, nobody will see anything." He worked the straps of her bra down over her shoulders and removed it, leaving her shirt open at the front and her breasts bare to his eager touch. He circled her nipples until they thrust proudly erect, then lowered his head to let his tongue tease them until they tingled.

"Todd," she whispered, "please . . . we must not—"

His hands became wildfire, scorching her flesh with flames of desire, and her body could not hide its response. Her breath was shallow and rapid, her nipples upright and throbbing. When she felt something warm and melting in the center of her being, she moaned aloud. Todd found her thrusting breasts with his mouth and sucked them to a pulsing readiness, the nipples warm and sweet under his tongue.

He felt his own passion rise, quickening with an undeniable urgency, and he lifted his head to study the shoreline once again. A boat drifted nearby, too close to ignore, and he cursed under his breath.

"What's wrong?" Roxie asked in a dreamy voice.

"There's a boat out there headed this way." His fingers slipped down her waist and found the zipper to her slacks, then tugged. "We don't have time to—"

Roxie turned her head to see the boat, brushing a kiss across Todd's cheek as she did so. Even though the boat was getting nearer, Todd's fingers continued their intimate journey. "Don't, Todd," she whispered. "We need to go now."

"Let me do this for you first," he insisted, his fingers repeating their lingering caress.

Roxie reached out blindly to stop his hand. "No, not this way, not unless it's for both of us."

"Are you sure?" He knew she was near the breaking point.

She nodded fiercely.

He pulled her against him and gave her a quick, hard kiss. "In that case, let's get out of here." They hurriedly straightened their clothes, and Roxie rolled her flimsy bra into a compact ball and stuffed it in her hip pocket. She found the sandals she'd kicked off earlier and put them back on for the trek across the burning sand.

They'd just emerged from the sand dune and started down the beach hand in hand when a female figure approached. "Damn, it's Jocelyn," Todd muttered. "I'll have to figure out some way to get rid of her."

"There you are, darling," she cried. "I've been looking everywhere for you." When she got close enough to get a good look at them, Jocelyn could tell immediately that sparks were flying between Todd and Roxie. "How cozy, darling. I see you found someone to entertain you."

"This is Roxie Lyons," Todd said ungraciously. "And Roxie, this is . . . Jocelyn Kendrick."

"Lyons? How very interesting," Jocelyn said. "I suppose George Lyons is your father, then? Surely he's not your husband, is he, darling, though I dare say he's terribly rich."

"I suppose he's rich enough," Roxie retorted. "And yes, he is my father."

"Why, Todd, how clever of you." Jocelyn was too skillful to make a crass accusation, but the insinuation that Todd was pursuing Roxie for her father's money hung in the air. Jocelyn's eyes swept over Roxie and acknowledged her beauty, though of a rather full-blown type compared to Jocelyn's own delicate platinum coloring. Roxie was competition, however, and Jocelyn wasn't quite ready to let go of Todd. She would have to nip this romance in the bud. "Have you had enough of this party yet, or do you need a little more time?"

A vein throbbed in Todd's temple. Jocelyn's behavior was even more outrageous than he remembered, and he was so furious that he had to shove his hands in his pockets to keep from forming fists. He had to get rid of her before she did any more damage. "Let's get out of here," he said, grabbing Jocelyn's elbow and pushing her toward the road. "I'll call you later, Roxie."

"Just a minute," Roxie shouted. When Todd turned around, she stomped across the sand toward him. "What's going on, anyway? You were getting ready to go back to Dallas with me, remember?"

Jocelyn couldn't conceal the smug smile on her face as she watched Todd and Roxie glare at each other.

"I forgot about Jocelyn. I'll have to take her home."

"What about me?"

"Can't you go back in your own car? I'll meet you later."

"I don't have my car here. I came with Daddy and Lorraine."

Todd was so angry that he couldn't think straight. "I don't know what to do, then. I don't think it'll do for the three of us to go back together."

"Why, darling, I have no objection to a *ménage à trois*," interjected Jocelyn.

"Well, maybe *you* wouldn't, but *I* do!" Roxie said. "I couldn't bear to watch the way you work on Todd and try to tear him down. When you got through with him the last time, there was nothing left. He was like . . . like one of these pieces of driftwood washed up by the tide. Wasn't that enough for you? Won't you be satisfied until you have him completely broken and useless to himself or anyone else?"

"Oh, really, this is too, too melodramatic," Jocelyn answered. "Let's go before we draw an audience with all this ill-bred shouting." She turned her back and started toward the road.

"Just a minute." Roxie was so mad that she was crying, and she dabbed at the tears until mascara streaks trickled down her cheeks. She grabbed at Jocelyn's elbow and whirled her around, then impulsively pulled back her hand to strike. Just in time, she caught a glimpse of Jocelyn's shocked expression. "Oh, hell," she said. "It isn't worth it. If Todd doesn't have sense enough to know what kind of person you are, then he deserves you." Roxie shoved past Jocelyn, leaving Todd behind. "I'm going back to Dallas with Daddy. Don't bother to call me until you figure out what it is you're looking for."

Todd watched Roxie stalk across the sand, her tiny hips swaying with each step, and felt a startled admiration for her. Beside him Jocelyn cleared her throat. "My goodness. That was certainly a nasty little scene. Are you ready to go, darling?"

"Maybe you can find a ride with someone else, Jocelyn."

"Oh, I already tried, darling. I was going to ride back with Julian and Rusty, but Mr. Lyons called them over and spoke to them, and then they told me they won't be able to take me home after all because they have to do an errand for him."

"An errand for the boss on Labor Day?"

"I thought it was strange, too, but he's a high-handed old man. He just ruined all my lovely plans. Rusty and I were getting on so well, you know."

"I don't suppose George noticed that, did he?"

"He might have, darling. Rusty was making quite a fuss over me."

"Well, you've had yourself quite a day, Jocelyn. Seems that everybody made quite a fuss over you." Todd snorted bitterly. "Come on. I'm taking you home . . . to pack."

Chapter Twelve

Todd doodled on a scratch pad and wondered if the clock had stopped. It must have been at least five minutes since he'd checked the time, yet the second hand hadn't budged. It was October 1, and an executive session was scheduled for three o'clock to announce the winner of the contest.

The office had been a madhouse yesterday, with a flurry of paperwork and last-minute telephone conversations. Todd hadn't left the office until midnight, when the contest ended, and neither had Julian and Rusty. The accounting staff was still hard at work when they left, trying to feed all the data into the computers. The accounting manager had said it would take another day or two to prepare a final report, but George had bellowed loud enough to be heard in Fort Worth, and the accounting people volunteered to work all night and get the job finished. Today there had been so much running back and forth to check entries and decipher handwriting that everybody's nerves were on edge. At two o'clock there still hadn't been a final computer run, but the harried accounting manager promised to have it ready by three. He said it was the best he could do.

Todd looked down at the preliminary totals he'd kept on his own production and felt confident that he had won the contest. Unless he had drastically underestimated the projects Julian and Rusty had done lately, he knew he would overcome their earlier momentum and squeak past the finish line ahead of them. Then he and Roxie would be married and that would be the end of the matter.

He got up and paced the room, tension fraying his nerves until he couldn't be still. September had been the hardest month of his life. He'd come back from the Labor Day picnic with Roxie's words ringing in his ears: "Don't call me until you figure out what it is you're looking for." She'd meant it, too. When he tried to call her, she asked him if he'd made up his mind what he wanted, and when he began to stammer, she hung up on him.

He'd known all along that he didn't want Jocelyn, and he didn't want his apartment, either. It was a constant reminder of those terrible months when he'd hurt all the way to the marrow of his bones. Before nightfall on Labor Day, he'd packed his clothes and personal things, given Jocelyn enough money to last a month and wished her well, then moved to the Adolphus while he waited out the contest.

He still didn't have an answer to Roxie's question,

though. He wasn't sure any more what he wanted. He was gun shy and skittish, disillusioned with love. He didn't love Roxie and didn't want to. He'd never again let himself be vulnerable to a woman the way he'd been with Jocelyn. He'd had quite enough of love and its heart pangs, thank you very much.

But even if he didn't love Roxie, he wanted to marry her. They could have a good life together, because in addition to the sparkle and fizz of their physical chemistry, they shared an ambitious interest in the company. They were a dynamite combination, and Todd knew it.

Roxie had complicated things by letting herself get confused over the difference between love and infatuation, but she was as smart as she was beautiful, and she'd soon figure it out. She'd eventually realize as he did that life was simpler, happier and less dangerous without love and its snares. In the meantime he'd win the contest and her hand in marriage, and they could begin a triumphant march into the future. Todd could almost hear the sound of trumpets. He tossed his pencil on the desk and looked at the clock again. Five more minutes . . .

Roxie couldn't seem to get rid of the choking sensation in her throat, and her heart fluttered in her chest like a bird's. She'd tossed and turned all week, worrying about this moment, and every time she'd tried to talk to Daddy, he'd brushed her fears aside. He'd refused to give her a single hint about how he would handle the meeting today, preferring to speculate that Todd would win the contest.

Maybe in George's mind it would solve all their

problems if Todd won, but not in Roxie's. She didn't intend to marry Todd just because he won the contest, and tried over and over to convince George of that fact. Sometimes she wondered if he tuned her out when he didn't like what she said. She meant it, though. This time Daddy wasn't going to get away with humoring her until she capitulated. She didn't quite trust him to keep his word and had made her own plans. She took a deep, shaky breath and crossed her fingers for luck. She was going to need it. . . .

The conference room was as noisy as a children's birthday party and felt charged with electricity when Roxie swung open the door. Her eyes swept the group of officers and found Todd standing alone near the window, a drink in his hand. They exchanged glances, and Todd lifted his glass in a salute. Roxie was quickly surrounded by the other officers, who joshed in a merry way about the contest and kept referring to the "big day." Rusty had bitten his fingernails down to the nubs, and Julian looked sophisticated in a black suit with crisp white-on-white shirt. A perceptive appraisal, however, revealed dark shadows under his eyes.

Roxie turned back to Todd. There was a touch of fall in the air, and he was wearing a camel's hair jacket with charcoal gray slacks. As usual his shirt was open at the neck, his tie loosened, as though he'd been working hard right up to time for the meeting. Funny, he can't stand anything tight around his neck, Roxie thought, realizing that she'd almost never seen him with his collar buttoned up, his tie knotted properly. He needs room to breathe. He'll never be uptight like Julian.

Roxie let someone pour her a cup of coffee while she straightened the bright scarf at her neck. She was wearing her teal blue Halston dress for the first time since April, the day they'd launched the contest. It seemed appropriate to end the competition in the same dress. Besides, this meeting was going to be a real challenge, and she needed to look her prettiest. She twisted a topaz ring with nervous fingers and wondered why Daddy wasn't there yet. It was time to start.

George rushed through the door, a sheaf of papers in one hand, his white hair mussed. Roxie moved quickly to join him and whispered an urgent question. "Daddy, you'll tell them first thing the contest is cancelled, won't you?"

"Roxie, please, let me handle this," he insisted, brushing her aside. "These are only the preliminary figures. Accounting still doesn't have the final report, and I don't know who won the contest. I'm just going to have to play it by ear."

"But, Daddy, it doesn't matter who won the contest," she whispered urgently. "I'm not going to marry the winner, don't you understand that yet?"

Before George could reply, others had joined them and someone clapped George on the back, congratulating him for the record-breaking surge in company profits over the past six months. He beamed with pride, Roxie temporarily forgotten. Everyone took their places at the conference table, unable to keep their eyes from the folder in George's hand. Who had won? The way the lead had shifted from month to month, it could be any of the three vice-presidents.

"All right, everybody, let's get started," George

said, rustling his papers and fumbling in his pocket for his glasses.

Roxie took another deep breath and stood up. "Before we get started, there's something I'd like to say to all of you." Everybody turned to her in surprise, and George tried desperately to wave her back into her seat. She ignored him and continued, her voice a little shaky. "This is the hardest thing I've ever had to do, because I've always prided myself on being a person who keeps her word."

"Roxie," George shouted, "please sit down."

Something prickled down Todd's spine, and he knew by the expression on Roxie's face that she'd decided to call off the contest, just as she'd told him she wanted to do that day at the lake. So she really meant it when she said she would be a reluctant bride if she had to marry the winner of the contest! Todd felt all his plans turn to dust, and an unbearable cramp in his middle.

"I realize now that I made a terrible mistake when I dreamed up this contest and agreed to marry the man who made the biggest profits for the company in a six-month period," Roxie continued. "I looked on marriage as a business arrangement where two people combine their assets in order to make more money. I'd never been in love—" She paused and her trembling gaze made its way to Todd, who sat with his head in his hands and didn't see her.

George seized upon the momentary lull. "Thank you, Roxie, and now we'll get on with the meeting." If she was determined to call off the contest, why, then, they'd call it off, but not like this. As emotional as Roxie was right now, she'd get everybody all stirred up in the wrong way and set the company back ten years. If he could get her to sit down, he'd take care of it himself—the right way.

But George failed because Roxie was determined to do this herself, and she disregarded his urgent signals while her soft voice continued. "I didn't believe in love any more than I believed in Santa Claus. But I was wrong. And now I have to ask you to forgive me, because you've all worked so hard all these months. I don't know if you'll ever be able to understand, but please try, won't you?" Her blue eyes pleaded with them, and she looked so stricken there wasn't a man in the room who wouldn't have snatched out his own heart if it would ease her suffering. "To my complete surprise," Roxie continued, "I fell in love, for the very first time, and even though I hate to go back on my word, I can't marry the person who won the contest, no matter who he is."

Julian and Rusty exchanged amazed glances. They'd monopolized her time so completely that there wasn't room for another man in her life. Who could it be?

Todd lifted his head in an unspoken question. If she loved him as she said she did, then why couldn't she marry him when he won the contest? Why did she have to call it off? It didn't make sense.

Roxie had to raise her voice in order to be heard over the startled exclamations of her listeners. "I've come to realize that it's impossible for me to marry someone unless he loves me the same way I love him." She paused and glanced again in Todd's direction, then plunged on. "I've given a lot of thought to whether I should resign from the company. After all, my decision to withdraw from the contest may cause some hard feelings. But I love it here. I've done everything I can to help build something we can all be proud of. I can't give it up, not unless you force me to."

She waited for their reaction and was relieved when she heard a chorus of nos.

"There's no way I can thank you for your support and for the way you've pitched in and worked so hard," she continued. "I hope you'll understand that this is what I have to do. I feel that the winner should receive something more than my apologies, so I've decided that in addition to the 5 percent of the company stock which Daddy agreed to give the winner, I'm also going to give him the 5 percent which Daddy promised me."

Roxie wasn't really surprised to hear herself giving away the money. It was important, but not as important as the people who made up Sunshine Enterprises. As she saw it, forfeiting the prize was the only way to maintain the kind of employee morale that would keep the company spiraling upward.

George yelped in pain. Something had ripped a hole right through his pocketbook, and he felt two million dollars slide away, lost forever. If he'd given that company stock to Roxie and her husband, it would still have been in the family. But to give it to an employee, just because he won a contest . . . now, that was something altogether different. Roxie, how could you? he moaned under his breath.

But George had to silence his whimpers because the group broke into spontaneous applause. Roxie had done the generous thing, the magnificent thing, in fact the only thing that would keep the company intact after this mortal wound she'd dealt it. George was shrewd enough to recognize that truth, and he managed a weak smile.

"Thank you, Roxie, and now if you'll please sit down," he said with a vigorous, impatient wave of his hand, "I'll take charge of the meeting."

Roxie's eyes were watery as she turned her glance to each of the corporate officers. In one quick gesture she reached across the table and shook hands with Julian, Rusty, then Todd, murmuring a polite word of thanks to each. Nodding to her father, she sat down, grateful to have gotten through the ordeal before her knees buckled.

"As Roxie said, the winner will now get 10 percent of the company stock," George said, rolling with the punches. "Will someone check to see if the accountant is here yet with the contest results?"

There was an expectant hush in the room as the accountant hurried in, his eyes bloodshot, his face stubbly with an extra day's growth of beard. He liked to do things in an orderly fashion, and this race against the clock had left him completely drained. "Here you are, Mr. Lyons," he said, handing a computer printout to George. "Of course we'll have to go over everything again and verify all the figures—"

"Thank you, William," George interrupted. Accountants could be such a pain with their persnickety ways. "Why don't you all go home now and get some sleep? We appreciate your spending the night here to do this so we could know immediately who won the contest. Tell your staff they'll find a little something extra in their paychecks this month." George clutched the papers with his liver-spotted hands, wishing he could've had the results a little earlier. He hated to learn the winner of the contest at the same time as everyone else, without time to plan how to break the news.

The accountant moved soundlessly across the carpeted floor and closed the door with a slight whoosh behind him. He thought again, as he had so many times before, that George Lyons really didn't have the slightest idea how the Accounting Department functioned. How did he think William could send everybody home early, when all these figures had to be verified? The overtime costs would be astronomical! It would completely ruin his departmental budget for the month. William took an immaculate handkerchief from his vest pocket and patted his forehead. He couldn't go back to his staff with perspiration on his face.

Roxie forced her fingers to be still, her lips to smile, as George unfolded the stack of sheets to find the column with the grand totals.

Todd turned in his chair and looked out the window at the Dallas skyline. So she had really done it; she had pulled out of the contest. She didn't care who won, and all those months of effort to prove himself to her had been for nothing. All at once Todd didn't care whether he won the contest or not. He'd only wanted to win because of Roxie. The money had ceased to matter a long time ago, and winning twice as much wasn't going to fill this void in his heart. The prize he'd striven for so mightily was her hand in marriage.

He turned to look at her, so beautiful in her blue

dress, her eyes misty, her lips tremulous as she returned his gaze. The reluctant bride would never be his.

A tidal wave of grief and loss washed over Todd, leaving him pale and shaken. The pain he'd suffered at losing Jocelyn was nothing compared to what he felt now, and he bit his lip to hold back an anguished cry. Why had he been so blind? He'd lied to himself about his reason for wanting to marry Roxie. It had nothing to do with ambition or money or even sexual attraction. The truth couldn't be simpler. He loved her.

Instinctively he started to rise and go to her, but George interrupted his action. "Let me find the page with the grand totals," George said, peering through the half-rims of his reading glasses. "Here it is." He paused and sucked in his breath, then said in a surprised roar, "And the winner is Rusty Wales! Congratulations, Rusty." George scrambled to his feet to shake Rusty's hand, with the others right behind him. Rusty's normally pink complexion had deepened to beet red. Beside him Julian looked wan, though he managed a dismal smile.

George shouted into the hubbub, "Rusty, you crossed the finish line almost a million dollars ahead of everybody else. Nobody else was even close." He rattled off the figures for Todd and Julian, and the profits he gave for Todd were within a few dollars of the total on the scratch pad in Todd's office.

How could I have underestimated Rusty so much? Todd wondered as he shook the winner's hand. I had no idea his latest projects were so profitable.

It took a couple of minutes for Todd to grasp the reality of the rapidly changing situation, and then he grinned in delight. Thank God Roxie had withdrawn from the contest when she did. Otherwise she would have had to marry *Rusty!* Todd had been angry with her because he'd assumed he would be the winner himself and that when she backed out, he had lost her. Now she was free, and he could marry her after all, just as soon as he convinced her that he was in love with her. He found her standing at the fringes of the crowd, a speculative look on her face as she saw him start toward her.

His smile was bright enough to light the entire room, and Roxie completely forgot the crowd when Todd pulled her into his arms. "I want you to be the first to know that I've finally figured out what I'm looking for," he murmured, holding her face between his hands as he brushed her cheeks and eyes with tiny kisses. "The only thing I really want is you, Roxie. I love you, my darling." His lips pressed hers in a long, sweet kiss that left them both breathless, and when they pulled apart, their curious colleagues began to clap and cheer.

"So this is the reason you wanted to call off the contest," Rusty said in surprise. "And all the time I thought you and Todd hated each other." Rusty pumped Todd's hand with enthusiasm, happy enough at his own victory not to begrudge one to Todd. Roxie gave Rusty a big hug, but a jealous Todd soon pulled her back to the warmth of his own arms. They both shook hands with Julian, who seemed a little dazed and, for the first time in his life, at a loss for words.

"Daddy's going to have to do something for Julian, too," Roxie whispered. "Do you think we can talk him into giving Julian a percentage of the stock?"

George, who was standing close behind them, overheard their remarks and clutched his wallet. Roxie would give away the whole damn company before this was over. When she turned toward him with an ingratiating smile, George shook his head. "Two percent, Roxie, and not one cent more," he insisted. "I have to save something for my grandchildren, you know."

"Speaking of grandchildren," Todd said, a boyish grin on his face, "don't you think we ought to get married right away so we can get started on our new assignment?"

"The sooner, the better," Roxie answered.

When Todd bent his head to kiss her again, George wandered away. It was no use to try to talk sense to them when they were in a mood like that. By the time they'd finished their kiss, George was contemplating his future with a grandchild on each knee. He looked back over his shoulder and saw that they were kissing again. Maybe he'd better plan on a whole passel of grandchildren, the way they were going at it. He smiled with real happiness. Growing old wouldn't be so bad with youngsters around. But they were going to need a grandma, too. He lifted his head and grinned. Where was Lorraine, anyway?

He eventually found her taking rapid-fire instructions from Todd, something about plane reservations to Albuquerque and a Jeep, while Roxie looked on in amazement. "Daddy," she whispered, trying to listen to Todd while she was talking, "I think he's lost his mind. He said we're going to get married today in Santa Fe because we can get married in New Mexico without having to wait for a blood test."

"Get married today?" George cried. "Elope to Santa Fe? But, princess—" George's protests were cut short, because Todd turned toward them and scooped Roxie into his arms.

"Let's go, beautiful. There's a plane in thirty minutes, and if we hurry, we can make it."

"But, Todd, I don't even have a suitcase," she said, her eyes wide with wonder.

He reached in his pocket for his charge cards. "I have these," he said. "We don't need anything else." Todd turned to George and gripped the older man's hand. "Sir, I want you to know that I love Roxie very much, and I intend to spend the rest of my life trying to make her happy. She's the best thing that ever happened to me, and I think I'm the luckiest man on earth." He put one arm around Roxie's waist and hugged her against him. "I hope to make you proud of me, George."

George felt something tight in his throat that made it difficult to swallow. So he was going to lose his baby girl at last . . . but to such a fine young man that he really couldn't complain. If he'd picked a husband for her himself, he couldn't have done a better job. George threw his arms around the two of them and blinked back the tears. It was time to let go.

Chapter Thirteen

𝒯heir plane touched down in Albuquerque in less than two hours, and because they'd flown into the Mountain Time zone, they gained an hour. It was only five o'clock in New Mexico when they rented the Jeep Wagoneer which Lorraine had ordered by telephone for them, and headed north into the Sangre de Cristo mountains. The cool mountain nights had already turned the foliage the brilliant golden hues of autumn, contrasting vividly with the white trunks of the aspen. Roxie thought that there must be a hundred different shades of green, ranging from the silver green of the sage to the blue green of the spruce to the yellow green of the yucca. The roadside was carpeted with yellow, pink and purple wildflowers, and the sky was the intense blue found only in high, arid altitudes.

They passed through tiny towns with huts of Mexican adobe and historic churches from early settlement days. Every church had a carefully tended cemetery with bright flowers at each headstone, and most of them also had schools. Strings of bright red peppers hung at every porch or doorpost, serving a decorative as well as a practical purpose. The air was thin and clear, full of the scent of cedar and pine, and there was no sound except the purr of the engine, the hum of the tires against the pavement. Roxie lay her head against Todd's shoulder and feasted her eyes on the beauties of nature.

"Happy?" he asked, brushing her hair with a kiss.

She answered him with a radiant smile, too moved to express her joy in words.

"Sure you won't change your mind?"

"Well," she said teasingly, "this has been rather sudden." Todd's expression clouded, and she quickly added, "No, darling, of course I won't change my mind. I love you too much. Besides, I think I'd better grab you while I've got the chance. I'm not sure you won't change *your* mind."

"Never," he said, driving with one eye on the road while he kissed her soundly. Fortunately the narrow road was almost deserted, and nothing was endangered when Roxie parted her lips and the Jeep swerved with Todd's sudden reaction. "Now, now," he scolded gently. "If you don't behave yourself, I'm going to pull into these woods and you aren't going to become a respectable married woman until tomorrow."

"Respectability, pooh," Roxie said, stroking his thigh. The Jeep swerved again, and Todd pulled onto a convenient dirt road arbored with evergreens.

"Todd, what are you doing?" Roxie cried in feigned alarm as he pulled her into his arms and buried his face in her neck.

"Exactly what any other red-blooded male would do in the same circumstances," he answered as he found her lips and greedily devoured them. His hands instinctively made their way to her soft curves, caressing her through the heavy suede fabric of her dress. "Damn," he muttered, searching for the buttons, "I can't even feel you under this stuff."

"I can feel you," she whispered, teasing his skin with stimulating strokes of her fingers.

"There's more of me already," he said hoarsely, holding her face between his hands while he plundered her lips.

"So I notice," she answered, her breath coming faster with excitement. "Oh, Todd, darling," she said softly as his hand slipped inside her dress to fondle her breast. Her mouth sought his in an urgent kiss that brought their desire to fever pitch.

Behind them a car honked, and Todd lifted his head and shook it, trying to clear the dizziness from his brain. "Damn," he said, when his eyes were able to focus again, "we're blocking the gate. This is a private road."

"Can they see us?" Roxie asked, straightening herself on the seat.

"No. The seat back is too high. Hold on, sweetheart, because we're going to back out of here and burn up the road to Santa Fe. We're getting married right now and put an end to these cruel interruptions." The tires on the Jeep squealed as Todd threw it into reverse, then slammed into low and sent gravel pinging against the undercarriage.

They reached the outskirts of Santa Fe within fifteen minutes, and Todd threaded his way through the narrow streets to the town square. He made a few inquiries of people at the courthouse, made a telephone call, and in almost no time the court clerk arrived, opened the office and issued a marriage license. Todd expressed his gratitude with a generous tip that made the clerk happy she'd come back after five o'clock to reopen the office for a rich Texan. They found a justice of the peace nearby who was equally happy to oblige them and asked whether they wanted the marriage ceremony performed in Spanish or English.

"Spanish is a more romantic language," Roxie said.

"I want you to understand what you're promising," Todd answered firmly.

The small-boned Mexican justice of the peace turned his head from Roxie to Todd. "If you prefer, we can have *both* languages, señor."

And so, shortly after seven o'clock on the night of October 1, Roxie and Todd exchanged their marriage vows in two spoken languages, but were bound together for eternity by the unspoken language of love. When he finished the words required by the state, the justice of the peace made the sign of the cross and said, "God bless you," in both Spanish and English. He smiled and nodded, his weathered skin crinkling with pleasure, and rocked back and forth on the balls of his feet while Todd kissed his not-at-all-reluctant bride.

"I love you, Roxie," Todd said in a hushed voice, "for now and forever."

"And I love you, my darling." Her smile was so dazzling and so full of trust that Todd felt the prickle of tears and turned his head to blink them away. As long as he lived, he would remember the way she looked today, her eyes blue and sparkling, her face radiant with love. Even when her tawny hair turned silver, he would love her just as much as he did now.

"I bet you'll be a beautiful old lady," he whispered.

"I bet you'll be a handsome old man," she whispered in return. "Are you sure you know what you've let yourself in for?"

"It's too late to do anything about it now—except die trying," he said, grinning. He peeled off a large bill and handed it to the little Mexican man, then scooped Roxie in his arms and rushed her through the door while the two hired witnesses pelted them with rice.

They went on a wild shopping spree with Todd's charge cards, finding a number of stores open late to accommodate tourists. They got the essentials first, groceries, toothbrushes and a razor, then casual cottons with a comfortable look which belied their expensive designer price tags. Last of all Todd found a lingerie boutique and with only a slight reddening of his ears bought Roxie a sky blue gown and negligee of sheer, filmy nylon lavished with lace. In a state of extravagant euphoria, he bought two other nightgowns, one black, one peach, then whispered against her ear that he doubted she'd need them.

"But think how nicely they'll decorate the bedpost," she replied, holding one of them against her body to check the daring plunge of its neckline.

Todd signed the sales slip, suddenly eager to be done with shopping. "Do you need anything else?" he asked.

"Only you, my darling," she whispered.

Todd answered with a low growl that made Roxie feel a sudden churning in the pit of her stomach. "Come on, let's get out of here."

"Where are we going?" Roxie asked, propelled forward by his firm grip on her elbow.

"That's a surprise," he answered, unlocking the Jeep and tossing in their bundles. "And it's going to take almost an hour to get there, so I suggest you take yourself a little nap. If you keep doing what you were doing on the road from Albuquerque, we'll have to pull over and spend the night in the car."

He handed her into the Jeep and slammed the door, then headed north through the mountains again. The sun set in the spectacular wash of scarlet followed immediately by blackness. Roxie was too excited to sleep, but she curled up on the seat beside Todd and tried to imagine where they were going. By the time he cut off the main road onto a heavily rutted dirt one, she'd lost all sense of direction and could see nothing except the beam of the headlights falling on the road ahead. The Jeep began to climb a steep, narrow track that seemed to lead almost straight up the side of a mountain, but Todd would say nothing more than "Santa Barbara Canyon."

Within the promised hour he braked the Jeep to a stop and opened the door to the crisp, cold air. "Here we are," Todd said, tousling Roxie's hair. "Home at last."

"Home?"

"This is my cabin. I bought it last year," he replied. "Here, let me carry you across the threshold." He lifted Roxie's slight body in his arms and took three long steps across the driveway, then fumbled with the key until the door swung open on rusty hinges. He reached inside and flipped a light switch, then bent to kiss Roxie's lips. "I didn't know one person could make me so happy," he said. "I love you, Roxie, my darling wife. Welcome to my home and my heart." He carried her inside and kicked the door shut behind them, then lowered her to her feet and pulled her into his arms for a long, tantalizing kiss.

"It's cold in here," she said, shivering even in the warmth of his arms.

"I'll build a fire and warm you up in nothing flat," he said. "Or would you rather wait?" His grin was teasing even as his fingers worked with the buttons on her dress.

"Is there a fireplace?" she asked, looking around the cabin for the first time. "Oh, Todd, let's have a fire," she exclaimed when she saw the stone fireplace. "It will be so romantic."

The cabin was old but well kept, with a large room that served as both den and kitchen. A stone fireplace covered one entire wall, and there was a rack of logs ready to start a fire. Todd expertly arranged several logs, then shredded some old newspaper and struck a match.

While he worked the bellows, Roxie went into the only bedroom and plopped onto a feather mattress. It was the softest bed she'd ever seen, and she tested it by bouncing up and down on it. Not a sound, she noticed. She went into the adjoining bathroom, simple and clean, and found a stall shower but no tub. Big enough for two, she noted again. She opened the cheerful curtains and peered out the window. Except for tiny flickering lights from cabins far down the mountain and the silvery glow of the moon and stars, there was total darkness outside. Roxie hugged her arms about herself and beamed. What a perfect spot for a honeymoon, she thought. For the first time, Todd and I are completely alone, with nothing and nobody to interrupt us.

"Todd, where are you?" she called in sudden impatience. It was time to get started on those grandchildren for Daddy.

Silhouette Special Edition

MORE ROMANCE FOR
A SPECIAL WAY TO RELAX

$1.95 each

2 ☐ Hastings	21 ☐ Hastings	41 ☐ Halston	60 ☐ Thorne
3 ☐ Dixon	22 ☐ Howard	42 ☐ Drummond	61 ☐ Beckman
4 ☐ Vitek	23 ☐ Charles	43 ☐ Shaw	62 ☐ Bright
5 ☐ Converse	24 ☐ Dixon	44 ☐ Eden	63 ☐ Wallace
6 ☐ Douglass	25 ☐ Hardy	45 ☐ Charles	64 ☐ Converse
7 ☐ Stanford	26 ☐ Scott	46 ☐ Howard	65 ☐ Cates
8 ☐ Halston	27 ☐ Wisdom	47 ☐ Stephens	66 ☐ Mikels
9 ☐ Baxter	28 ☐ Ripy	48 ☐ Ferrell	67 ☐ Shaw
10 ☐ Thiels	29 ☐ Bergen	49 ☐ Hastings	68 ☐ Sinclair
11 ☐ Thornton	30 ☐ Stephens	50 ☐ Browning	69 ☐ Dalton
12 ☐ Sinclair	31 ☐ Baxter	51 ☐ Trent	70 ☐ Clare
13 ☐ Beckman	32 ☐ Douglass	52 ☐ Sinclair	71 ☐ Skillern
14 ☐ Keene	33 ☐ Palmer	53 ☐ Thomas	72 ☐ Belmont
15 ☐ James	35 ☐ James	54 ☐ Hohl	73 ☐ Taylor
16 ☐ Carr	36 ☐ Dailey	55 ☐ Stanford	74 ☐ Wisdom
17 ☐ John	37 ☐ Stanford	56 ☐ Wallace	75 ☐ John
18 ☐ Hamilton	38 ☐ John	57 ☐ Thornton	76 ☐ Ripy
19 ☐ Shaw	39 ☐ Milan	58 ☐ Douglass	77 ☐ Bergen
20 ☐ Musgrave	40 ☐ Converse	59 ☐ Roberts	78 ☐ Gladstone

$2.25 each

79 ☐ Hastings	87 ☐ Dixon	95 ☐ Doyle	103 ☐ Taylor
80 ☐ Douglass	88 ☐ Saxon	96 ☐ Baxter	104 ☐ Wallace
81 ☐ Thornton	89 ☐ Meriwether	97 ☐ Shaw	105 ☐ Sinclair
82 ☐ McKenna	90 ☐ Justin	98 ☐ Hurley	106 ☐ John
83 ☐ Major	91 ☐ Stanford	99 ☐ Dixon	107 ☐ Ross
84 ☐ Stephens	92 ☐ Hamilton	100 ☐ Roberts	108 ☐ Stephens
85 ☐ Beckman	93 ☐ Lacey	101 ☐ Bergen	109 ☐ Beckman
86 ☐ Halston	94 ☐ Barrie	102 ☐ Wallace	110 ☐ Browning

Silhouette Special Edition

$2.25 each

111 ☐ Thorne	129 ☐ Rowe	147 ☐ Dalton	165 ☐ Lee
112 ☐ Belmont	130 ☐ Carr	148 ☐ Gordon	166 ☐ John
113 ☐ Camp	131 ☐ Lee	149 ☐ Claire	167 ☐ Hurley
114 ☐ Ripy	132 ☐ Dailey	150 ☐ Dailey	168 ☐ Thornton
115 ☐ Halston	133 ☐ Douglass	151 ☐ Shaw	169 ☐ Beckman
116 ☐ Roberts	134 ☐ Ripy	152 ☐ Adams	170 ☐ Paige
117 ☐ Converse	135 ☐ Seger	153 ☐ Sinclair	171 ☐ Gray
118 ☐ Jackson	136 ☐ Scott	154 ☐ Malek	172 ☐ Hamilton
119 ☐ Langan	137 ☐ Parker	155 ☐ Lacey	173 ☐ Belmont
120 ☐ Dixon	138 ☐ Thornton	156 ☐ Hastings	174 ☐ Dixon
121 ☐ Shaw	139 ☐ Halston	157 ☐ Taylor	175 ☐ Roberts
122 ☐ Walker	140 ☐ Sinclair	158 ☐ Charles	176 ☐ Walker
123 ☐ Douglass	141 ☐ Saxon	159 ☐ Camp	177 ☐ Howard
124 ☐ Mikels	142 ☐ Bergen	160 ☐ Wisdom	178 ☐ Bishop
125 ☐ Cates	143 ☐ Bright	161 ☐ Stanford	179 ☐ Meriwether
126 ☐ Wildman	144 ☐ Meriwether	162 ☐ Roberts	180 ☐ Jackson
127 ☐ Taylor	145 ☐ Wallace	163 ☐ Halston	
128 ☐ Macomber	146 ☐ Thornton	164 ☐ Ripy	

SILHOUETTE SPECIAL EDITION, Department SE/2
1230 Avenue of the Americas
New York, NY 10020

Please send me the books I have checked above. I am enclosing $_____
(please add 75¢ to cover postage and handling. NYS and NYC residents please
add appropriate sales tax). Send check or money order—no cash or C.O.D.'s
please. Allow six weeks for delivery.

NAME _____

ADDRESS _____

CITY _____ STATE/ZIP _____